The Truth About Thérèse

Henri Ghéon

The Truth About Thérèse

An Unflinching Look at Lisieux, the Little Flower, and the Little Way

SOPHIA INSTITUTE PRESS
Manchester, New Hampshire

The Truth About Thérèse was formerly published in 1934 by Sheed and Ward, London, under the title *The Secret of the Little Flower*, using Donald Attwater's translation from the original French. This 2011 edition by Sophia Institute Press® includes minor editorial revisions.

Copyright © 2011 Sophia Institute Press®

Printed in the United States of America

All rights reserved

Cover design by Carolyn McKinney

On the cover: Photograph of Thérèse dressed as Joan of Arc, © Librairie Thérèse de Lisieux, Office Central, Lisieux France.

No part of this book may be reproduced, stored in a retrieval system, or transmitted in any form, or by any means, electronic, mechanical, photocopying, or otherwise, without the prior written permission of the publisher, except by a reviewer, who may quote brief passages in a review.

Sophia Institute Press®
Box 5284, Manchester, NH 03108
1-800-888-9344
www.sophiainstitute.com

Nihil obstat: Edward Mahoney, S.T.D, *Censor Deputatus*
Imprimatur: + Joseph Butt, *Vicarius Generalis*
Westmonasterii, February 1934

Library of Congress Cataloging-in-Publication Data

Ghéon, Henri, 1875-1944.
[Secret of the Little Flower]
The truth about Thérèse : an unflinching look at Lisieux, the Little Flower and the Little Way / by Henro Ghéon. — [Rev. ed.].
p. cm.
Originally published: The secret of the Little Flower. London : Sheed and Ward, 1934. With minor editorial revisions and new foreword.
ISBN 978-1-933184-68-5 (pbk. : alk. paper) 1. Thérèse, de Lisieux, Saint, 1873-1897. I. Title.
BX4700.T5G52 2010
282.092 — dc22
[B]

2009041835

8th Printing

To my friend Jean Schlumberger,
a country neighbor of Sister Thérèse,
in memory of summers long ago

Contents

Foreword

by Philippe Maxence

In his preface to the English edition of Henri Ghéon's *The Secret of the Curé of Ars*, G. K. Chesterton noted that "the Catholic Church is much too universal to be called international, for she is older than all the nations." This mystery of the Church — here finding expression in the manner characteristic of that great writer — explains how it comes to pass that a book written by a Frenchman about a saint who was not only French but was also raised by Pope Pius XII to the rank of secondary patroness of France should be reprinted today in the United States.

Its reader — even the one who may have opened its cover by chance — sees from the very first pages that he has to do with a writer in the truest sense, and that he runs no risk of plunging into the reading of a book that will leave him indifferent or that will simply parrot the tired, syrupy words of the old lives of saints. For in those opening pages, Ghéon ranges himself against Ernest Renan (1823-1892), who in the France of the 1930s still enjoyed a kind of moral authority among those who thought that progress had rendered Christianity outworn and reduced Christ to the status of merely one hero among many.

Renan, a former seminarian, belonged to that generation of men that was as much troubled by modern philosophy as it was by the growth of the experimental sciences. It was a generation that failed at the task of putting into an order the various claims of knowledge that were endlessly assailing them. Their faith, austere yet often sentimental, was unable to endure its hour of confrontation with the conclusions of modernity. Nevertheless, with the passage of time, the human heart — as a Pascal might say — took its revenge. Several years before the conversion of the author of this book, Renan's own grandson converted after having descended to the very pit of human misery. The brilliant Ernest Psichari (1883-1914) returned to the Faith not only with a profound adherence to the dogmas of the Church, but also with the desire to make reparation for the blasphemies of his grandfather and for his own father's misconduct.

This concern for the reparation that the Communion of Saints makes possible is not, however, what shaped the journey of Henri Vaugeon, Ghéon by his pen-name. To be sure, his pharmacist father was no believer. He belonged to the provincial French bourgeoisie that looked down its nose at a religion that it considered to be "an old woman's affair." All that we know of him, however, suggests that he was upright and a man of integrity. He never prevented his wife from giving a religious education to their two children, Henri and Marie.

Their childhood, therefore, was bathed in the gentle warmth of a religious sentiment that was reinforced each day by the family's evening prayers and every week by the ceremonies they all attended, dressed in their Sunday best. Yet in the years of adolescence, of boarding school, and of first love, this uniquely sentimental religion was of no use. For although the affections had been fully nurtured, the intellect had been abandoned like a desert, and the will had not been formed at all. The pious pleasures of an untroubled childhood were incapable of long resisting the call of senses that demanded their due. Because he had been able neither to perceive the truth that is to be known nor to will the good that is to be accomplished, young Henri had in his soul only affections to be satisfied. It was then that he plunged into that perpetual lack of satisfaction that belongs to the insatiable appetite of the flesh.

His friendship with the writer André Gide (1869-1951) settled him on a path in which the unbridled quest for pleasure was paradoxically associated with high intellectual standards. A poet and a literary critic, Ghéon participated in the 1908-1909 foundation of the *Nouvelle revue française* (New French Review), which at length established itself as the preeminent intellectual forum of the day. While some of its founders posited pleasure as the supreme obligation of their existence, they did not accept it as being the only rule of literature. From the journal's first issue, Jean Schlumberger — the one to whom this little book would be dedicated many years later — expressed this idea by writing that "where the exaltation of the artist knows no rule beyond his own pleasure, one finds only unrestrained expression and inner struggles."

Will the reader pardon my so insisting upon the subject of literature in a book devoted to a saint? We must come to the point: *The Truth About Thérèse* is the work of a writer whose personal journey sheds much light upon the book's unique character. The mistrust of "pious literature" that Henri Ghéon expresses from the very first chapter rests largely upon his own retrospective regard toward a childhood whose Christianity was too sentimental to allow him to confront the world and its snares with a well-nourished faith. The admiration that he avows for holiness in general — and, in particular, for the paradoxical Thérèse — leads him to demonstrate that literature and holiness are not mutually exclusive. In its own realm, true literature possesses in itself a standard of perfection that one also finds in the realm of sanctity. What is more, this standard of literary perfection allowed him to grasp the truth of Thérèse Martin, whose "little way" of gaining God more quickly he showed to be strong and, in a sense, virile. "She did not call for mawkish veneration," he explained. Nor did she "put forward a soft and feeble example; everything was strong; she was of the stock of Catherine of Siena and Joan of Arc, and her 'little way' was a heroic way — nothing less than plenary love of God and total surrender to Him."

It was while serving as a military physician during the First World War that Henri Ghéon rediscovered the Faith, on December 24, 1915, confronted as he then was by death, human misery, tragic losses, and the absurdity of a life without deep meaning. When later he returned to writing — but now as a Christian writer — he could not produce a precious portrait of the one who had so often been the recourse of the rugged soldiers in the trenches. The publication after the Second World War of the autobiographical manuscripts of the saint has vindicated Ghéon's approach. The manuscripts show that the little Carmelite was very much of her own time in the choice she made of images to describe the spiritual life, but that she also belonged to all ages, because she was, as Pope Pius XI put it, "a living word of God." Henri Ghéon captured her secret magnificently: like a true poet he went straight to the very heart of the mystery of Saint Thérèse of Lisieux.

Philippe Maxence is editor-in-chief of the Catholic journal *L'Homme Nouveau* and the author of numerous books, including *Pour le réenchantement du monde: une introduction à Chesterton* (2004) and, most recently, *Maximilien Kolbe: Prêtre, journaliste et martyr, 1894-1941* (2011).

The Truth About Thérèse

Chapter One

My Initial Resistance to St. Thérèse

It needs more than intelligence to understand holiness, more than sensibility to recognize it, more than a nicely balanced judgment to criticize it. A whole lifetime can be spent in the study of the Church's wonders, of spiritual books, and of the manifestations of sanctity without coming anywhere near its hidden reality. Indeed, to look at it in that way, from the point of view of a research-worker or of a *dilettante*, is a sign of complete blindness in its regard.

Now that I am on the threshold of the marvelous life of Sister Thérèse of Lisieux, I find myself face-to-face with the great M. Renan. He looks me up and down, he pities me. He is fully aware of the superiority given him by his learning, his ecclesiastical training, his subtle art, and his apostasy. He tends to think himself infallible and is not afraid to prophesy. He still has a certain taste for religious matters, but of religious experience he has retained only the affecting memory of a rather sickly emotional state, which gives his writing that greasy quality we call "unction." According to him, the Catholic religion is only a form of sentimentalism, and so, with its rites and its music, its poets and its heroes, it must submit to the law of all such and be assigned its place in a museum of grand and alluring anachronisms. Here, in company with the temples of ancient Egypt and the Homeric poems, with the enchantments of Shakespeare and the daydreams of Rousseau, it will be a source of pleasure to the curious and the aesthetic. The Church has had its day, and he accepts this fact. Even holiness is not spared his mournful condemnation; hear M. Renan: "Holiness is a kind of poetry which, like many others, is finished and done with."

Then he adds, rashly, "Rome will go on canonizing saints [of course; isn't that her business?], *but there won't be any more canonized by the people.*"

Soon after that — so soon that he might have known her personally — the little nun of Lisieux was being acclaimed by the whole Catholic world, without waiting for the verdict of the Father of the Faithful. But M. Renan was dead, so he did not have to acknowledge his mistake.

When learned men make expeditions into the realm of souls, they should remember the saying of Christ to the woman of Samaria as He sits at the water-springs which they think they have sealed: "If thou didst know the gift of God . . ."[1] Holiness is "a kind of poetry" that wells up endlessly, for its source is not in literature, or in fancies, whether of the heart or of the senses, but in the very womb of the God of Life.

We would have to go back to the heroic ages of Christianity to find another saint so spontaneously and unanimously acclaimed and so quickly recognized by the Church as Sister Thérèse. She attained the altar almost before she was in the waiting-room; the intervals that Rome requires before confirming the virtues of even

[1] John 4:10.

the best qualified of her children were shortened for her, and only fifty years elapsed between her birth in 1873 and her glorification in 1923. For the last twenty years of this half-century, the whole world, its heart full of joy and its hands of gifts, had hailed her and called upon her with unparalleled steadfastness. And to the question: "What great events, what heavenly favors, what miracles, prophecies, visions during her life account for this extraordinary popularity?" the answer is: her silence, her obscurity, her very inexistence. She lived hidden, unknown except to a few friends and relatives, and to her dying day, her apostleship remained a secret within the walls of a convent. That is the greatest, the clearest, and the most overpowering of her miracles, or of the miracles done on her behalf. There is no purely natural explanation to be found for the acclamation she received. Moreover, no such explanation would suffice; not even, in my opinion, *The Story of a Soul,* that record of her confidences which was translated into almost every language the day after her death.

I don't want to underestimate its value or importance or influence, but, whatever energy was expended in making it known, whatever appeal it has made to souls, whatever its material success throughout the Christian world, could this humble little book, in outward appearance so like innumerable other "pious books," have had the power to raise such a tide of fervor and enthusiasm, to set a match to so many fires, or rather mines, going off all at once in every quarter of the inhabited globe, unless God had a hand in it? The first and sufficient cause of the popularity of this child was that God Himself slipped a rare grace between the pages of her book, like a pressed flower that has not lost its fragrance, a grace immediately efficacious and capable by its very presence of opening hearts to her teaching. But, if it is a matter of grace, is it not simpler to suppose that God acts directly on the featureless crowds of those who must be led, enlightened, and directed? Perhaps it was decided in the counsels of the Almighty Wisdom that not only should no lesson from the pen of Sister Thérèse be wanting in its effect, but also, and above all, that her sufferings, sacrifices, and prayers, the treasury of love and expiation of her short life, should all be poured out again, and poured out at once, over this needy world. Persecution was rife, war was coming on with giant strides. We were threatened with terrible trials for soul and body, and we hungered and thirsted after these graces.

A girl dies when she is twenty-four years old at a small Carmel in the heart of Normandy — a province not noted for its mysticism. The people there live well and drink better. Trouville is a couple of yards away, and Deauville just beyond, where the Prince of this world is in charge and has already become dram-seller on a large scale to the peasants as well. The body of Sister Thérèse was taken to the municipal cemetery, accompanied by a few friends; nobody else took any notice. The grave was scarcely filled in when the fragrance of her goodness found its way out. Everybody began to talk about her, first in one province, then in another, in France and all over Europe, in the Old World and in the New. Her name was on the lips of believers and infidels, those who could still say the name of Christ and those who had forgotten it. Why should she have been chosen when there were so many others who had died about that time whose virtues had been demonstrated concretely and in public, servants of the poor, missionaries, apostles, martyrs, godly men and women of all kinds? "Thérèse! Sister Thérèse!" It was all Thérèse.

But what had she done for us during her life? Anything we could see? Anything we could touch? Nothing. Or nothing that we knew anyway. And yet everybody was calling to her. It was enough that she had said, "I will spend my Heaven doing good upon earth." That saying was snatched up, repeated, broadcast. But could it be believed? It was believed; it had to be. Why did it have to be? That is a matter of love, and love cannot be explained.

Before going any further, I have to make an admission. I have begun to venerate the second Thérèse only lately. Moreover, I am writing this book primarily for all those, Catholics or not, who resist her attraction, as I once did. It is difficult not at once to make common cause with a unanimous verdict of the faithful; on the other hand, a delayed acquiescence gives time for reflection and allows the mind to make a less superficial examination of her whom we are asked to regard as holy. Not that I claim to say anything new, however trifling, on a subject that has already received so large a tribute of ink, but the confession of my personal experience may be useful to others.

At first I knew Sister Thérèse only by the statues of her. Obviously, the sight of crudely colored and mawkish plaster figures could not entrance a new convert who, even in his faith, was full of futile aesthetic prejudice. In those days I looked to the Church for beauty as well as for truth; I had yet to learn that truth is essential but, so far as this world is concerned, beauty is not, however helpful it may be to prayer . . . Then I read *The Story of a Soul.*

I don't know whether I came to this book too soon or too late. It did not bore me — but it did not captivate me; here and there it irritated me (may I be forgiven!). At the first reading, I was not attracted or moved or even instructed. It may be that I was still incapable of appreciating the worth of "the little way" that it teaches, but it is more likely that I had already found it for myself in the lives and writings of other saints, or simply in the Gospels themselves, for they teach it in every line. Spiritual writers only restate in words, and saints only relive in deeds, those things which Christ said and did; and His saying and doing are incomparably better than theirs, in accordance with the inherent perfection of His being. When He said, "Unless you become as little children," He pointed out the "way of childlikeness" of Giles the abbot and the Poor Man of Assisi and the Curé of Ars and Germaine the shepherdess. Thérèse of the Child Jesus comes after them, does what they did, and restores to its place of honor this primordial teaching that we are prone to neglect.

One of the principal duties of the saints throughout the ages is to incarnate anew, to dress in contemporary clothes, such ancient truths as are likely to be overlooked precisely because of the appearance they have worn too long. So we see St. Francis dress himself in sackcloth, M. Vianney in a moth-eaten cassock, Thérèse Martin in a First-Communion frock of the fashion of 1885 — and an astonished world suddenly recognizes the humbleness, the poverty, and the innocence that have for twelve, eighteen, nineteen hundred years been visible although not always seen beneath the white tunic of our Lord. So Thérèse taught me nothing about simplicity, renunciation, and childlikeness that had not already been shown me by St. Germaine, St. Giles, St. Francis, St. John-Baptist Vianney, and many others. If I had read her book to the end, it might have taken hold of me; unfortunately, I let it slip from my fingers.

I was neither disappointed nor sorry. I reminded myself that we must revere all the saints, but that among so many we are free to exercise a preference and to choose specially certain ones according to our time and country, our position and age, our character and temperament. Thérèse was not for me. I could not deny that she was for my time, but on this point I was not of my time. The tinseled and sugary manifestations of devotion to the "*little* saint" (the abuse of this diminutive drove me frantic) had successfully hidden from me the greatness and perhaps originality that was surely hers. There were too many roses, too many flowers of all sorts. I could see nothing but roses; a few thorns underneath them, of course, but then any saint without thorns is an impossibility. I reverenced her in her statue — from afar.

However, her miracles made me think a bit. I knew sick bodies that she had cured, souls that she had changed, scholars who knelt at her feet, persons of high spirituality, used to the heights of St. John of the Cross and the first Teresa,[2] who nourished themselves on her words. I saw that she was the refuge of very dear friends who came to Christ only through her or lived in Him better by her. It required a strong effort for me to try again. I went at last to Lisieux, *The Story of a Soul* under my arm, resolved to see everything, to read everything, and to dare everything — even the chapel of her shrine.

I know that I am now going to upset many people, and I apologize in advance. But I must point out the stumbling-block that is in the way of persons like me; if I don't, they will not follow me and I shall have failed in my object. The others might be shocked by me, but their convictions about St. Thérèse will remain unharmed. And that is what matters.

The chapel of the Carmel at Lisieux is at the end of a narrow courtyard and has a frozen look outside. On entering, one strives hard to find some attraction in it. Were it plainer, it would not be

[2] St. Teresa of Avila (1515-1582), Spanish Carmelite mystic.

half-bad; there is a crushing excess of ornament, as useless as it is bad, yet this might be overlooked. But on turning to the right to venerate the holy relics, we are at once up against the masterpiece of hideousness and stupidity that has the high honor of sheltering them. The pseudo-renaissance cupola and its worthless stained-glass windows are the least of the absurdities. The shrine itself is showy, clumsy, quite without beauty: let that, too, pass. And I am not particularly offended by the brocade and velvet with which the recumbent image of the saint is dressed up in its gold and crystal cage. Certainly it would be preferable for this flesh-aping marble, polished, tinted, "idealized" beyond words, to be habited in woolen serge; but then in Italy and Spain, the most obscure martyrs can be seen covered with jewels and glittering fabrics like stage princesses: they are in glory, so why not glorify them?

What I cannot tolerate are the shrine's supernatural guardians, two gigantic angels and a child musician: they are carved so flabbily in a marble so white and soft that they seem to melt like sugar while you look at them; the child has a harp in one hand and a flower in the other, and with the flower he plays the harp. To complete the crime, the sculptor (doubtless an "eminent" one) has set out on the steps several things like marble-sugar in the form of scattered roses and — to crown the horror — from a dense oily cloud there rises a ponderous bronze cross. I will not dwell upon the decoration of the walls, pale-blue "draperies" made of stucco and dripping with roses in relief. The uniform spirit of the repository, pretentiousness, jingling poeticalness, and pious adulation give a confusing unity to the whole thing. The Madonna by Bouchardon, a little affected but good, which hangs at the back and once smiled upon the saint, is hardly noticeable amid its expensive surroundings. And remember that this gilding will never be dulled, this stucco never fade, this marble never lose its shiny surface — for the lighting of candles is forbidden; bulbs of electric light have superseded them. We are among the new rich, whose drawing-room furniture has cost too much not to be kept like new.

It would be laughable, if one could find the heart to laugh. It makes the visitor ashamed of his country and of his century, ashamed that he lingers among such enormities. He feels the spirit of the image-breakers rising within him. He is sorry for Thérèse and asks her forgiveness for these outrages . . .

Shut your eyes. Recollect yourself. Think. Forget that sculptor; forget those who, with the best possible intentions, gave him his orders and directed his hand. Smell the real roses that cover the floor; they are fresh every morning. Catch the fragrance of goodness that somehow breathes from those bones. Be humble about your likes and dislikes, humble yourself even to the extent of accepting ugliness . . .

Our reason persists: why does God allow it? Why does Thérèse allow it? Why has God let the Devil have this triumph, that this holy place should be in the front rank of monstrosities of Catholic ecclesiastical art in the twentieth century? Does the soul no longer inform the body, and the spirit the flesh?

After a long time of reflection and resignation, it must be conceded that the *cultus* of Sister Thérèse is associated with other external things besides these. There is also in Lisieux a superb cathedral. There is the touching house Les Buissonnets. There is the cemetery, with its little enclosure for the Carmelites, on an apple-covered slope in the greenest of the valleys. Above all, there is the devotion, the true devotion, of the humble folk who fill and transfigure the chapel at every hour of the day. In the presence of that lowly child and of her God, these deformities and insufficiencies, the images, rosettes, and pious ditties do not matter. They are only a means; prayer goes far beyond them. Yet the surrender we are longing to make must wait for one more argument: Was all this stuff really necessary? Could we not have done without it?

No. Probably we could not. Those of us who are put off by it are only a small minority. Thérèse was given to her own times; humanly speaking and in her earthly aspect, she was made a standard for them, and the devotion she excites has taken the external form that it required. If it was to find its way gently to the burning secret of her soul, her age had to have this unreal display — the cheap scents, the romantic poetizing, the Christmas-card roses, the statues akin to the marble groups that adorn the more expensive hotels. We need not try to explain it away, for it does no wrong to Thérèse. The Lisieux way of doing things, the taste of her devotees and of the worthy nuns who cultivate "accomplishments" in honor of their sister, was her own, that of her family and of her "world." Where and when could she have learned anything better? It is supreme everywhere throughout Europe and America, and is lovingly fostered by a huge *bourgeoisie*. Its reign is far from over, for it makes headway among the mass of the people and successively contaminates each new level of the middle-classes. It cannot be denied that most people like it. God bequeathed it to Thérèse — and she uses it.

I do not mean to say that we have the saints we deserve; we never deserve the saints we have. But we are given the saints whose outward appearance is most likely to attract us. Are souls, then, to suffer because appreciation of art has been withdrawn from society through the fault of the *bourgeois* Republic? Jesus Christ did not die for artists and men of good taste alone; they can go to Chartres, and some of them will come back converted. The crowds that descend on Lisieux and carry away its trash as well as its graces to the ends of the earth find themselves quite at home; everything there astonishes and delights them. The atmosphere of complete at-homeness invites their enthusiasm and confidence, until they are free, without knowing it, from the pretty-pretties that have led them on. As they pray, they find the real Sister Thérèse underneath the sugar roses and cheesy clouds, behind the platitudes and pet-names that take all the salt out of her most heroic story: Thérèse, the ascetic of the wasted body and bruised heart and unbending will, whose sacrifice was ceaseless, who lived on and died from a love that was all pain. That is what lay behind her smile; I have read *The Story of a Soul* again, and it is beyond question. Some jam must be mixed with the powder if the multitude is to take so bitter a medicine. She mixed a little herself. The convent of Lisieux has added more, perhaps too much; but doubtless they did well, since so many faithful souls have found the physic palatable.

I am speaking for the others, those who are sickened by the jam, deterred by the sham art, driven to flight by the rain of roses; and for their sakes I erase the garlands from the margins of the book of her unutterable confidences, take that distressing pastry sniff away from the walls of her chapel, reject the photographs that have been touched up, deliberately or involuntarily, to "give her a more suitable expression." I wish that I could go further and display in these pages nothing but her consumed and conquering soul — the equal in warmth and energy, if not in poetic genius, of that which made another Teresa the glory of Spain: its superior, if *superior* be the word, in firmness, even hardness — for, to my judgment, the first Teresa had a greater tenderness. But I cannot write only of her soul, because, to make her comprehensible, she must be put back into her fleshly integument and shown in her own time and place, among those lower-middle-class folk who provide the means by which she pleases them and whom, by a fair exchange, she recalls to their highest duties. To this I must resign myself, and my own origins are an advantage, for I resemble Sister Thérèse of Lisieux in that I was born of the *petite bourgeoisie*, in a provincial town, and at about the same time. If I had never left that town, perhaps I should have shared the taste in religious art of her family, her convent, her followers — in other words, her own. It might be better for me if I did.

Chapter Two

A Spoiled Child

Approaching Alençon from the railway station by the rue Saint-Blaise, there is to be seen on the right-hand side a fine sixteenth-century mansion with a courtyard in front; it was formerly the townhouse of the Guises and is now the residence of the chief administrative official. Opposite it on the other side of the street is a small house, also built of brick and stone but as modest as the other is grand; yet with a certain style about it. Its front is broken on the ground floor by a door and two windows, and on the upper storey by three nicely bowed French windows opening on to an iron balcony. When too freshly painted, the house looks like a new toy. A modern chapel, reminiscent in its false elegance of the one at Lisieux, fails to spoil the whole. It was here that Thérèse was born.

Visitors are courteously welcomed by a charming old lady who lives in the house and looks after it with the greatest care. She is the widow of a Scots clergyman who received an inward intimation from the saint that he was to enter the Roman Church. At the end of a flagged passage is the narrow, steep staircase, with polished mahogany handrails, where the little girl used to count each step and stop every time to call to her mother until she answered. There is a marvelously fresh atmosphere about the big downstairs room where Mme. Martin used to sit by the window, designing patterns for the precious lace that was made for her by outside workers. That same spotless white curtain filtered the light onto her work and guarded the recollection of her prayers; she would have tempted the brush of van Nicer of Delft. At the back, a movable glazed partition still cuts off the dining room, and at celebrations, this partition would be opened to make room for the extra leaves of the oak table, which were necessary when the whole family was to sit down together.

There may be a few alterations in detail, but nothing has grown older; Thérèse's times are still our times, for in this quiet corner of France, things move very slowly. All the furniture and appointments are ordinary, solid, and simply designed; everything keeps its spirit: it is held there by a prayer. Passersby are few, and there is a great weight of silence, the unalterable quietness of the provinces; they say that it hides plenty of wickedness, but it certainly collaborates with God in the making of saints.

I suppose it is necessary for me to mention the room in which Thérèse was born, sacred to a wedded love which ever sought to be nothing but a duty. It is upstairs, behind the elder sisters' bedroom, and somebody has had the pious idea to connect it with the adjoining chapel. It is a shock, as one goes toward the flickering lamp that burns before the altar, suddenly to discover on the other side of a grating a sort of furniture-exhibit, in the style of the Tottenham Court Road before the emergence of the so-called modern style (which is not much better). In a dazzling light and against a blinding background is upreared one of those great old-fashioned beds which, comfortable and dignified no doubt, are yet neither beautiful nor ugly and emphatically demand a decent dimness. This one has no respect for tradition. It shows off, preens itself, flaunts its new clothes: the counterpane, canopy, and curtains are of currant-red silk plush, decked out with pompons. A window with a lace blind and more currant-red curtains backs it up, and two chairs (one a child's) and an empire table are disposed around.

In the presence of such an outpouring, the imagination collapses. The relentless decoration kills the smiling Madonna whose haloed picture hangs under the canopy above the bed. The walls are freshly repainted, and so tell us nothing; the parquet floor, scraped or relaid, does nothing but shine with polish — it looks as if it had never been trodden by a human foot.

We are a long way from M. Vianney's room as it is kept at Ars. And, I may add, we are a long way from the room in which Thérèse Martin first cried aloud before Heaven. The piety of that date was capable of results less scandalous than this; here its aberrations have reached their limit, and I shall not refer to them again. But it must not be forgotten that the germ of these things was in the Martins themselves and affected their daughter from her cradle.

Nevertheless, M. and Mme. Martin were not in all respects like their neighbors. They shared the tastes, prejudices, and habits of their class on many points, but as Christians, they were rather different. I do not mean that religion was a matter of complete indifference to their fellow-townsmen. Thanks to centuries of experience, to their natural earnestness, and to constant contact between town and country, the people of the western provinces of France have long been fortified against the propaganda of "new ideas." Under the July Monarchy and the Second Empire, the Church took her bearings and regained almost all the ground that the Revolution had taken from her and which the Empire and the

Restoration had tried to recover by politics rather than by conviction. In spite of the crimes of official dechristianization, there can still be found in the French countryside not only isolated rocks of religious enthusiasm but also, as it were, great alluvial deposits, scarcely covered with sand, wherein the convictions of their forbears endure and only need a turn of the plowshare to bring them to light. The middle-class people of Alençon were practicing Catholics. At Corpus Christi, they hung flags outside their houses, and officials regarded it as an honor to carry the canopy at the procession; the men went to the high Mass every Sunday, and most of them fulfilled their obligations at Easter; there were few "free thinkers" among them.

But Christians of the quality of the Martins were certainly rarer, and they were a cause of inverted scandal. The refrain is always the same: "They exaggerate" — there is nothing less bourgeois than exaggeration.

M. Martin's father came from Athis in the *département* of the Orne. He fought in Napoleon's wars and stopped on in the army after Waterloo, often changing his station. That is how the third of his children, Louis, came to be born at Bordeaux in 1824. When Captain Martin retired, he settled down at Alençon, not far from his birthplace, because it was convenient for his children's education. He was as good a Christian as he was a soldier and never trifled about duty; everything had to be exact, and he would allow no deviation from rules. This piety that he passed on to Louis may well be called military, and with it went a soldierly bearing that his son never lost.

Louis was a tall upstanding fellow, always looking straight before him; at twenty, he was the handsomest young man in the place. But he was never a soldier. He went to some cousins at Rennes, and there he adopted Breton dress and became a clock-maker, perfecting himself under a friend of his father at Strasburg. This quiet and precise trade suited him well; it encouraged him to meditate on the shortness of life. He had a poetical turn of mind, and his childhood's habit of looking at everything from the angle of eternity led to a liking for high places, where he could feel nearer to God and worship Him in His creation (he was especially fond of watching sunsets). Accordingly, when he was twenty, he set out for the Alps, traveling partly on foot and partly by stage-coach, half tourist and half pilgrim, until he came to the snow-clad solitude of the Austin canons in their monastery on the Great St. Bernard. He did not know enough Latin to be accepted there; so, with his father's approval, he decided to take up serious studies. They were stopped by sickness.

Then, disappointed but resigned to disappointment, he went back to clock-making and, after a short residence in Paris, opened a small shop at Alençon. It was in the rue du Pont Neuf, a few yards from the river. The name Martin can still be seen on the signboard, surrounded by watches and clocks and rings and necklaces, for later he added a jewelry business to his trade. Here he lived a bachelor's life until he was thirty-five.

People did not know what to make of this monkish watch-maker. He was good-looking, with a full well-kept beard, reticent in manner, educated; he never went outside his shop without putting on a frock coat and bowler hat. As he went about the street, he did not look at women, even out of the corner of his eye, and seemed to think as little about getting married as he did about recreation. When he found a man drunk in the gutter, he would help him up and lead him home. He was at Mass every morning, and his house was a meeting-place for several devout old men, who discussed with him the best way of helping the needy and sinners and of forwarding the work of missionaries on behalf of the kingdom of

God. This haunter of churches was so well thought of by everybody that he quite upset the accepted opinion that a man "given to good works" must necessarily be sour in disposition or a hypocrite. It must be added, to place him exactly, that he was a keen angler.

At this same time, there lived in the house in the rue Saint-Blaise already described a certain Mademoiselle Zélie Guérin, together with her old father (a retired police officer), her brother Isidore, and a sister. She was a local girl and had been to school at the Adoration convent. An irresistible sympathy for human sufferings had prompted her to seek admission among the Sisters of Charity of St. Vincent de Paul, but the superioress of the Hotel-Dieu had refused her, without reason given. Where Louis Martin had failed, so Zélie Guérin failed, too. This rather remarkable coincidence has not been invented afterward as a frill to a pious legend; those are the facts, solidly established. M. Guérin had very little money, so Zélie became a lace-maker. Thenceforward she could be seen at her window, putting together squares *of point d'Alençon* or making charming designs on paper for the discharge of the orders that came in such marvelous numbers. She wrapped herself in contemplation, and God was always with her. She mused on the possibility of serving Him more fully by marrying a husband who would be no less concerned for his glory, and bringing many children into the world who should be consecrated to his service.

These two craftsmen, the clock-maker and the lace-maker, lived in different parishes, and their families were not acquainted. The two did not know one another. They waited. How they met one fine day on St. Leonard's bridge, like Joachim and Anne at the Golden Gate; how he made way for her, and she passed him; how they looked at one another; how Zélie recognized unerringly that this was the companion intended for her by God: all this is a secret that Heaven has kept well. We only know that there was mutual understanding and delight, that the families met, and that the two were married. Louis Martin was careful for his own maidenhood and believed that it was his wife's wish, too, to shelter hers under the fine veil of a purely spiritual union; and there is documentary evidence that they lived together for a year as brother and sister, like St. Valerian with St. Cecilia. This awesome and superhuman paradox might have subsisted their whole lifetime, but Thérèse would not have been born, and it would seem that, in the plan of divine providence, this marriage had no other object. Zélie told her husband that she wanted children, that he and she should found a family of saints in accordance with his own desire. Her wishes were fulfilled: of her nine children, four went to God between the ages of six months and six years; the other five all became nuns.

For their first christening-name, all were called after our Lady, and there were successively Mary Louisa, Mary Pauline, Mary Léonie, Mary Helen, Mary Joseph Louis and Mary Joseph John Baptist, Mary Céline, Mary Melania Thérèse, and lastly she who was to be Saint Thérèse of Lisieux. Helen, Melania, and those longed-for sons, the two Josephs, who they had hoped would be missionaries, died in childhood. Of the surviving daughters, Mary Louisa, who by privilege of the firstborn was called simply Mary, was not quite fourteen when the youngest, Thérèse, was born.

Zélie Guérin's practical aptitude was as keen as her faith, and her lace-making business, which she had continued to carry on, became so prosperous that, in 1870, her husband gave up his own shop in order to help her with the increasing work; as his father was dead, there was nothing to keep him in the rue Pont Neuf. Meanwhile, war had broken out, and they underwent the miseries of the German invasion; had it not been checked, his age would not have prevented Louis from serving with the volunteers. His father-in-law also being dead, he inherited the house in the rue Saint-Blaise, and the family settled down there, where they lived for seven years. So we come back to the birthplace of the saint. I am reminded of the traditional account of the birth of our Lady from Joachim and Anne.

After the death of Mary Helen, when she was five and a half, Mme. Martin's sister, a Visitation nun at Le Mans, wrote to her with innocent simplicity:

> I can't help thinking that you're privileged to give these chosen ones to Heaven, where they will be your joy and your crown. And one day your unfailing trust and faith will have a tremendous reward . . . You may be sure that God will bless you, and the consolations that are now withheld will be the measure of your bliss. For if our good Lord is so pleased with you that He sends you the great saint that you have wanted so much to honor Him with, won't you be well repaid?

Msgr. Laveille, one of the best writers about Thérèse,[3] compares these words with those that Mme. Martin herself wrote to her sister-in-law at Lisieux when she had suffered a similar bereavement:

> When I have to close the eyes of my dear little children and follow their bodies to the grave, of course I am utterly miserable, but my sorrow has always been resigned. And I don't regret the trouble and care that they have been to me.

[3] Msgr. Laveille, *The Life of St. Thérèse of the Child Jesus*, trans. Fr. M. Fitzsimons, O.M.I. (London, 1928).

> Everybody says, "It would be much better if you'd never had them." I can't bear such talk. It doesn't seem to me that pain and difficulties can be put into the balance against my children's eternal happiness.

That letter shows the quality of Zélie Martin's faith. It is alleged that she often received graces out of the ordinary, so sensitive was her spirit — foreknowledge, supernatural advice, and enlightenment. And all the time she nursed her idea of giving a "great saint" to the world.

The two elder girls went to school at their aunt's convent in Le Mans. The third, Léonie, was delicate and a source of worry. Céline began to walk. Little Mary Melania died. There was no sign of the long-desired, perhaps promised, saint. Then, in 1872, another pregnancy raised fresh hopes, and again a daughter came to fill the empty cradle. She was born on January 3, 1873, when Mary and Pauline were home for the new-year holiday. Their mother's suffering kept them awake, until at midnight M. Martin tapped at their door and told them that they had a baby sister.

Next day, Mary Frances Thérèse Martin was christened in the church of our Lady. It is the most beautiful church in Alençon, with a triple gothic porch, strong and delicate, a very garden of carved stone: this was her doorway into the world of grace. The font whereat she received the spirit of God is in the first chapel on the south side, which has been thoroughly "restored" in the modern manner but less badly than any other of the neoteresian sanctuaries. Her eldest sister, Mary, was godmother, but the name Thérèse prevailed over the others.

The troubles of life began at once. Her mother could not feed her, so Thérèse was put out to nurse with a peasant, Rose Tallé, "little Rose," at Semallé, a few miles away. She nearly died twice, and malignant typhoid threatened the life of her sister Mary. Prayers and pilgrimages were undertaken for them, and both recovered. Spring completed the cure, and at four months, Thérèse weighed fourteen pounds; at ten months, she could stand upright and, by her first birthday, was walking by herself. Her mother thought she could discern destiny written upon the child's bright face and had her back home. M. Martin was making pilgrimages of thanksgiving to Chartres and Lourdes, and Zélie took more trouble than ever with the new baby.

The Martins worshiped their last-born. Everything she did was right, everything she said was clever, everything that happened to her was miraculous. When she was eighteen months, she clambered onto the swing, with no fear at all except lest she should not go high enough. She fell out of that big bed without hurting herself or even waking up — angels must have carried her. The fact was that her stay in the cottage at Semallé had made her a sturdy little peasant, proofed against hard knocks. She was good-tempered, lively, sensitive, and was passionately fond of her mother.

She would cry if Mme. Martin could not come into the garden with her; she would run out into the pouring rain to meet her coming back from Mass. The piety in which she was trained became in her equally violent and exacting. She would not leave out a word of her night-prayers: "That's not all," she was wont to say to her father; she had to "pray for grace," too.

"Dear little mother!" she exclaimed. "I wish you would die, because then you'd go to Heaven." That wish was fulfilled. And in her "exuberance of love," she wanted her father to die, too.

She got on well with her sisters. Mary was the serious one, who hoped to go back to the convent where she had been at school, while Pauline was the more gifted and steady and was, accordingly a little pleased with herself. Thérèse was less attached to Léonie, who was always ailing and difficult, although good-hearted and persevering. These were in her eyes the "grown-ups," who were to be imitated and envied and treated with respect. Her bosom-companion was the gentle charming Céline, who was devoted to her little sister. At getting-up time, Thérèse would slip into Céline's bed and snuggle down to her. When the nurse came to dress them, she was greeted one morning with the remark, "Go away, Louisa. Can't you see we're like two little white hens who can't be pulled apart?" The fowl-run and flowers and singing birds meant a lot to Thérèse, and she was able to absorb every sort of interest.

Mme. Martin did her best to restrain the extravagances of Thérèse's affection, but she often had to own herself beaten. I have alluded to her habit of going upstairs one step at a time, calling out, "Mamma!" at every one. Mme. Martin was expected to reply, "All right, my darling!" each time, and if she failed, Thérèse stopped where she was until the answer came. M. Martin called her his "little queen," played ride-a-cock-horse with her, and showered presents on her. Her collection of toys shows that in this respect, she was certainly spoiled, and for a long time she fancied that everything was hers by right; she had only to say, "I want it."

Thérèse was eager, intelligent, headstrong, and almost unbelievably stubborn; when she had said no, nothing could move her. Sometimes when her father wanted to hug her or her mother came to kiss her in bed, she pretended not to know them; she wanted them to want her. She was a woman. She liked to have her arms bare because she looked prettier that way, and she would pose to herself before the mirror. The story of the penny gives an idea of her *amour-propre*. Her mother told her that if she would kiss the ground, she should be given a penny. "No, thanks, Mamma. I'd rather not have the penny," replied Thérèse.

The importance of her childhood's exploits must not be exaggerated, although she has confided them to us; there was another side to them. She was not afraid to give trouble to her father and mother and to oppose them; that was in accordance with her high-spiritedness. The second stage was when her guardian angel moved her to self-reproach and shame and to beg pardon. Then she would cry for hours, and it was not easy to comfort her.

But there was one person whom she would on no account grieve when He came to her mind (and already she thought about Him a lot): that was the child Jesus, who was very much alive for her. She lived partly in the mysterious world of supernatural reality familiar to her parents. Once, when she was in the garden, she saw, or thought she saw, near the summer-house, "two horrid little spirits on the rim of a lime Alençon, dancing like mad, although there were iron chains on their ankles." They looked at her "with blazing eyes" and dived inside the barrel as if they were frightened; then they took refuge in the linen-room. Seeing they were so nervous, she looked in at the window to see what they were going to do. "The poor little demons were running about the tables not knowing where to hide from her eyes . . ." Was she calculating the strength of her innocence, and did she suppose she could overcome the Evil One without coming to grips with him? She did not yet know the oppositions within her own nature and the weapons that these could lend to Satan. At four and a half years old, this is not surprising.

The most disquieting feature of Thérèse's early childhood, referred to above, can hardly be overemphasized; it characterizes her, it sums up her temperament, her possible destiny, her actual destiny. The watchful Satan pounced on it and began to hope.

Céline and she were playing with their dolls, when Léonie came up with hers, "laid in a basket full of dolls' clothes, nice bits of stuff, and other desirable things."

> "Here you are," she said, "Choose."
>
> Céline had a look and took a ball of braid. I considered for a minute and then, exclaiming, "I take the lot!" I snatched basket and doll and everything.

Telling this incident fifteen years later Thérèse adds a devout reflection:

> When the way of perfection was shown to me I learned that to become a saint, a person has to suffer a great deal, always to look for that which is more perfect, and *to forget self*. I learned that there are many degrees in holiness and that each soul is free in its response to our Lord's invitation to do much or little for his love — in other words, *to choose* from among the sacrifices that He asks for. Thereupon I said as in my childhood's days, "O my God, I choose them all."

True enough; but it is not the point here. We have not yet gotten so far. We are trying to grasp the very human inner weakness of Thérèse's nature. Long before she was a saint, the little four-year-old, who seized the whole basket under the nose of her sisters, displayed a rapacity, an egoism, a spirit of conquest, in a word, an "imperialism," of quite remarkable energy; and this would one day have to be given an entirely new direction and transmuted into a tragical stripping away of self. It was a revelation, nay, an explosion, of Thérèse's nature, a nature that had to be broken-in like a thoroughbred to bit and saddle, if she was not to run the risk of being carried down to the depths of revolt rather than up to the heights of holiness. That cry of hers was not a

Christian cry; Nietzsche would have roared his approval; a limitless "will to power" was written all over it — and over her own authentic characteristics.

Look carefully at a photograph of St. Thérèse — not one that has been touched up and prettified or where she has been made to look soft and "ecstatic," for the least suggestion of pose is deceiving, but one of the snapshots where her face has been caught by surprise among her sisters in the cloister; better still, the most suffering and characteristic of three taken in 1897 in which she is holding against her breast images of the Holy Face and the child Jesus. The reserved smile, the gentleness, the serenity cast only a thin veil over the face of one who is firm and strong, tough and obstinate, imperative and victorious, who knows what she wants, who will want it until death, and who will not yield an inch from having her own way. *Fiat!*

As she was, so she remained. When she was four, her developing natural vitality "chose the lot," good and bad together. At the age of reason, this temper would have worked for evil had divine grace and her environment not been in the opposite scale. In the end — her spirit clarified by instruction, by prayer, and by the inpouring of the Holy Spirit — she chooses the good, all the good, the sovereign Good, the Absolute in all His fullness. We must not be blinded to the ambition that was the dominant note of her character by the means that she uses for overcoming it (they are of a disconcerting humbleness). Little by little, she traces her own will on the will of God. That is the drama of her life and the miracle of her destiny. Both are undervalued by the whittling away of the part either of earth or of Heaven in this relentless struggle; her story becomes commonplace, and her personal significance shrinks. It must be emphasized over and over again that Thérèse was not an obscure, sober little schoolgirl who, for small sacrifices, deserved the reward of being carried off suddenly amid a profusion of choice blossoms. She was a creature of passion and strong will, marked to be the prey of the pride of life; and Eternal Love subdued her without any lessening of her power and strength, and led her in the ways He willed.

Chapter Three

Pride Transfigured

Mary Martin had given to each of her sisters a special sort of rosary that was used by the pupils at the Le Mans convent to keep count of their "good deeds." Each time they voluntarily did without something they wanted, or helped somebody in distress, or kept their temper in trying circumstances, one of the beads could be separated from the rest and added to the string of self-denial.

Children are attracted by any devotional practice that is like a game and at the same time smacks of heroism, especially if, as in this example, there is an element of competition. So Thérèse, whose pride could not bear to be beaten by Céline, entered on the path of self-denial; she found that on these terms there was a certain pleasure in being good. The asceticism of these two small girls urged them to own up when they had done something wrong (or thought they had), to bear punishment without complaining, to refrain from justifying themselves at the expense of the real culprit when they were wrongly accused. They found all this exciting and thrilling, and it was not very difficult. The habit of self-sacrifice and going without became second nature, and they surrounded their virtue with a mysterious secrecy that increased its worth in their eyes.

One Sunday, Thérèse came back from a walk with a glorious bunch of wildflowers — and once she had gotten hold of anything, she did not easily let go. And now her mother, quite unconscious of how much she was asking of the child, claimed the bouquet for our Lady's May-shrine. Our Lady cannot be refused; one's mother cannot be refused. Thérèse gave it up. She did so with great unwillingness and sickness of heart, but her disappointment and her tears were hidden, and only Céline guessed them. In spite of her rather morbid sensitiveness, a time was to come when she would not even cry.

A few months after the death of her sister, Mother Mary Dosithea, who had taught the elder girls at Le Mans, Mme. Martin was struck down by a disease that she had kept hidden for sixteen years. Acute and increasing pain made her admit that she was suffering from a tumor in the breast. She was operated on, but it had been left until too late, and it only hastened the unavoidable end. Her strength was quite gone, and she had to resign herself to "giving up her lace and living on her investments." Would Heaven deny her the happiness of seeing her younger children grow up? Leaving them at home with their father, she joined a pilgrimage from Angers to seek health at Lourdes, where, in the overpowering heat of June 1877, she plunged four times into the icy water. She came back to Alençon worn out and murmuring the words of our Lady to Bernadette: "I promise to make you happy in the next world, but not in this."

As Mme. Martin gradually sank, Céline and Thérèse were boarded with a neighbor to spare them the daily sight of their mother's agony. The last time she got up was to "preside" with M. Martin at a make-believe prize distribution, arranged by Mary in her bedroom. Céline and Thérèse were dressed in white to receive the books and gilt paper crowns from their mother's hands. Viaticum was brought on August 26, and Thérèse was present at this last Communion and Anointing. Soon it was all over. Thérèse was dry-eyed when she kissed the cold forehead; but she stayed a long time by the coffin in the passage. She had not imagined that death could cleave so great a gulf. Nevertheless, she stood up to loss and grief; her small daily sacrifices enabled her to face more cruel ones without betraying her inward desolation. Quite apart from the action of grace and her absolute certainty of her mother's happiness in Heaven — had she not wanted her to be taken there quickly? — there was a vitality and essential joyousness in Thérèse that nothing could destroy.

When, after the funeral, their nurse poured out pity on the motherless children, Céline threw herself into Mary's arms, exclaiming, "You will have to be mother now!" But Thérèse was not so sure, although Mary was her godmother. She looked at the sad face of Pauline, who perhaps was a little jealous at having no one to look after, and said as she buried her face in her lap, "No! Pauline shall be mother!" Is it too early to see a spiritual significance in this new bond, so spontaneously fashioned? For it was Pauline who was to open the door of Carmel to Sister Thérèse of the Child Jesus.

They had to leave Alençon, that town of quiet streets hardly touched by commerce, with its humped little bridges over the Sarthe and the Brillante, its pleasant garden-bordered streams and pools, the pale severe walls in the market place, the solemn still churches, the gracious sedate life of the gray countryside. It is impossible not to love Alençon; its sole industry is a fairy game, and while it works its threads, it dreams and prays, and it induces others to dream and pray. It was the framework of her own daydreaming that Thérèse minded leaving more than anything else: the house, the square of garden behind with the swing and the fowl-run, the summer-house that M. Martin had hired to muse in undisturbed while the children larked around, the grass paddock where she loved to hide when the moon-daisies and cornflowers were in bloom — this "poetical" aspect of her nature must by no means be ignored. Soon she would be growing and unfolding in a neighborhood that is more rich and luxurious and therefore more sensual and disturbing to the will; but by that time, suffering would have done its work.

Mme. Martin's brother, Isidore Guérin, was a druggist at Lisieux. He had a wife as good as Zélie and several good-natured and well-brought-up children; he himself, after some youthful divagations, had settled down as a worthy man and a "militant" Christian. Mme. Martin, on her deathbed, had urged her husband to look for help and support from his brother-in-law's family rather than from relatives or friends in Alençon, and when he was asked, M. Guérin at once set himself to find a house for the Martins near Lisieux. It was called Les Buissonnets, and the children moved in before the end of the summer; their father joined them in November. Of all the places connected with Thérèse which are open to her devotees, this house is the most eloquent of her, the most intimate, and the least spoiled. Apart from the school hours with the Benedictines and the time spent on a visit to Rome, it may be said that she passed in it the whole time of her childhood and adolescence, from the age of four and a half to fifteen. With its two gardens, it was the most important factor in her formation and perfecting before she became a Carmelite. We find her footprints everywhere, hardly touched by our own.

But before the visitor can give himself to recollection without mishap, he has to stomach the sight of two disagreeable objects by which the garden has been dishonored. Near the gate, there is a clumsy cherub flourishing a shabby banner. And on the lawn behind the house, there is a quasi-photographic group in staring white marble representing Thérèse and her father, bigger than life-size, sitting together in a confidential attitude. This thing, which would be refused by a provincial town hall, is actually supposed to recall the hidden and heart-rending moment when M. Martin heard the first avowal of his daughter's vocation . . . The house itself has been respected, except that they could not resist turning the child's room into a chapel. This is nearly always done: it is the same with St. Catherine's room in the dyers' quarter at Siena, and with St. Benedict Joseph Labre's near Santa Maria dei Monti in Rome. This is not the way to bring us close to the saints and make them real. Surely it could be managed so that the honors given to them in the very place where they slept and woke, prayed and meditated, should at least safeguard the physical appearance of their private surroundings. In the present case, however, the distraction is lessened because the rest of the house is almost intact.

The road from Lisieux to Trouville is an expensive-looking boulevard. The visitor to Les Buissonnets leaves this road on the right, taking a shady footpath that winds upward among orchards and terraced villas until he reaches a door in a blank wall; it has stone steps and a small grating. This is it. Within, a curving graveled path leads through the sloping lawn and oval flowerbeds to the front of the house. It is a pleasant red-and-white villa, with an attic and two dormer-windows, surrounded by trees that are worthy of a district whose trees are royal. The garden at the back is rather higher, and half is given over to kitchen produce: there are cherry trees, currant bushes, and rows of peas, firs and spindle trees, more turf, and thick curtains of laurel and ivy suggesting secret passages and fine hiding-places. Against the washhouse wall somebody has reconstructed one of those tiny cribs that it gave Thérèse so much pleasure to build of pebbles and shells and bits of straw and wood; and a small plot nearby was "my garden," where she grew crocuses and blue periwinkles and ferns. Here indeed she can be seen and touched, and when you go into the house, she goes with you.

It is gloomy compared with the one at Alençon. The only authentic thing in the first room, which was the kitchen, is the redbrick hearth where the children put out their shoes on Christmas Eve. But on the right, one looks straight into the past: the dining room, an unimpeachable piece of evidence. This old-fashioned furniture has kept all its memories, and they agree with ours. Such furniture can be seen anywhere; we had foreseen it here; it had to be here. There is the sideboard with twisted columns, introducing (as is only fitting) two shooting trophies carved in oak, partridges, pheasants, and rabbits. Similar columns adorn both the tall, narrow armchairs and the dining chairs. There is a thick, round table supported on a single massive leg that blossoms out into four feet covered with acanthus leaves. The mirror above the fireplace would not be fulfilling its duty did it not reflect two glass chandeliers and a gilded bronze clock under a glass cover. On the walls there are two engravings "of the period," of ecclesiastical or biblical subjects, after David or Girodet. To crown all, impenetrable window curtains wrap everything in a semi-obscurity according to custom. It is a perfect harmony of the proprieties, a museum specimen of genuine nineteenth-century provincial middle-class comfort, in all its plainness and solidity, as it was displayed once for all in the place in which one ate. I am not laughing at it, for I find it rather touching. Granted the aesthetic premises, there is not a fault to be found with that room.

It is the same upstairs, in M. Martin's bedroom. I must admit that I like the mahogany furniture and the material of the bed-canopy and the curtains and the seats of the chairs, which makes one think of thick undergrowth of green, blue, and black leaves undisturbed by a breath of air. The room is dim and thoughtful, but not sad. The paneled one, where Thérèse lay at the time of her illness and was given back health of soul and body by a smile from our Lady, is cheerful and lightsome; white muslin curtains frame the recess where an altar now takes the place of a bed. It was the elder sisters' room. Previous to this Thérèse and Céline occupied the one at the back, level with the garden, in which statues and medals are now sold. There are displayed (under glass) her bed, her dolls and other toys, and the desk with the ebony and ivory crucifix which she used to question when she was doing her lessons. You can see her skipping rope, her shrimping net, her sailing boat, her dolls' kitchen, her draftboard, her cottage piano, her gift books, and her favorite bird's cage. It is a good thing to be reminded that she was once a child like any other and that her soul was, in its measure, nourished on the small things of childhood.

A special permission is required to go up to the attic-room. It was M. Martin's study and oratory, and he might be disturbed there only to give an account of the day's doings. It was, as it were, "a high place," sealed with blue and white panes, whereto the father withdrew to listen to the counsels of the Holy Spirit. It was his substitute for the Great St. Bernard.

That is a sufficient description of the house; the things that happened in it will fall into their right places of their own accord. Thérèse explored it with uncontrollable delight. With her thick hair flying and a black satin bow floating like a butterfly on her head, she ran about the garden, picked a belated gooseberry — then stopped suddenly, and her face fell. She went back with Céline into their room, fell on her knees, and burst into tears.

Her bravery was of short duration. She had restrained and hidden her sorrow so as not to sadden her father and as a test of the strength of her own will and faith. Then the journey from Alençon, the moving in, and the novelty of the new place had made her forget for a time. When she realized this, she did not spare herself: she called herself fickle, unkind, ungrateful to her mother, heartless. Her natural sensitiveness had been held in check for too long, and it overflowed; she cried and sobbed and abandoned herself as only an impressionable child can. This crisis passed, but the child who had been so lively and roguish and hard to please gradually became shy, gentle, and nervous, quiet and unobtrusive. She no longer wanted to have notice taken of her and would run away from strangers; simply to be looked at made her cry. That was the first thing that Lisieux did for her.

Mary and Pauline looked after the house; Léonie and Céline were day-scholars at the Benedictine convent. Thérèse had less time for play and went on with her lessons under the supervision of her "little mother," Pauline. M. Martin had aged a lot, and his hair and beard were already white. As he had retired, he could devote his whole time to his children and his hobbies and his religious life, and his day was regulated like a monk's: daily Mass at the cathedral, gardening, reading, Rosary, dinner, prayer before the Blessed Sacrament, at Notre-Dame or St. James or the Carmelite chapel of St. Desideratus, often with Thérèse, a walk by the river with rod and line, a call on M. Guérin, return home, supper, evening prayers with the family. Thérèse's time was divided in the same way between lessons, the garden and fields, and prayers. Religion was always with her: God wanted her to learn for His sake, to be good for His sake, to smile at beggars for His sake. For Him she built rustic altars and of Him she dreamed on the riverbank while her father fished. She would sit on the grass in some hidden spot, letting the multitudinous sounds of nature sink in; then the blare of a bugle from the barracks would recall her to the "world" and, in her own words, sadden her heart. She liked the rain as much as the sun; a thunderstorm right overhead pleased her; she would have bathed in dewy grass had not her sense of modesty held her back. A complete young pagan? Most certainly not. Such a one as poor Anne de Noailles, drunk with nature and earthly love, feels her limitations and can only fall into despair. Thérèse Martin can see further. This world contents her and disappoints her too, but for quite another reason — because it speaks of, prefigures, and at the same time *is not* Heaven.

Without morality, there can be no true mysticism, where there is no personal virtue, there is no prayer. Thérèse once hurt a poor man by offering him a penny as though he were a beggar. She thought that the cake she was just going to eat might be more acceptable to him, but did not dare to offer it for fear of another refusal. How could she reconcile sensitiveness with love? Then she recollected that she had heard that no gift is withheld on one's First Communion day; she would wait until that day came, and then she would pray for him. She remembered her resolution for six years and, when the time came, carried it out. To have a brotherly charity that neither grows slack nor dissolves into useless sighs is a trait among a thousand.

As the fields have their seasons, so has the Church. In his *Année liturgique*, Dom Guéranger, the restorer of Solesmes, has shown how every day they bring a fresh blossom or a new fruit to our daily prayer. On winter evenings, M. Martin was wont to listen to the reading aloud of this invaluable book, and so Thérèse learned to know the Christian seasons: Advent, Christmas, Lent,

Easter, Pentecost, with their changing hues of green, violet, white, and red, and the never-ending procession of saints across them. On Sunday morning, she found again the God of flowers and brooks and tempests in the solemn Mass at the cathedral church of St. Peter, where the family assembled in a chapel on the epistle side quite close to the high altar. It was there that a sermon, the first she could understand, showed her the God-Man nailed to the cross, suffering, dying, and she never forgot it. When, at six years old, she found herself inside a confessional for the first time — she was so small that the priest could not see her or she him — she had no difficulty in realizing that her God was there, for she knew that it was to Him that she was confessing. By grace and prayer the thought of God hardly left her mind; she was entering step by step into the reality of Christ.

Meanwhile, she was growing up; the woman began to show and to become aware of her own attractiveness. On Sunday evenings at M. Guérin's, she received a lot of notice and petting and small flatteries, for she was the living image of her mother. When she went for a short stay at Trouville, people used to stop her on the promenade to admire her brilliant eyes and smile and fair ringlets, and her popularity there might well have woken up a dormant coquettishness. But her self-respect and pride were too much for that; they had not weakened in the least and were playing in quite a different key.

One evening, she was walking back with her father from the Guérins, her eyes fixed on the stars in a sky of limitless depth. Presently she noticed "a cluster of golden jewels" forming the letter *T* — Orion's belt. She found this manifestation of the first letter of her own name an omen and very delightful (*"Quelles délices!"* is how she refers to her feelings when recollecting this occasion), and she stopped, exclaiming, "Look, Papa! My name is written in the sky!" This was not a child's joke; she firmly believed it. She could see no disproportion between the honor done her by the heavens and her diminutive person, and doubtless there was none between it and the spiritual ambition of her love. "I didn't want to look at the horrid old world anymore," and she asked her father to lead her home by the arm. She went into the house with her head lost in the stars, sanctified, blessed, canonized by her own self— that is, already filled with certainty that she would be one day. M. Martin entered into the game and did not for a minute consider rebuking her lack of humility; his daughter's presentiment agreed exactly with his own, and he was answerable for it. He lent himself with complete simplicity to what seemed to be God's will.

Holiness can be grafted onto pride, just as grace is grafted onto nature. There is a right pride as there is righteous anger. The last end of holiness is not so much a renunciation of the human personality as the possession of God.

Thérèse Martin can be left with what may still be called the illusion of future glory. It will soon be clear that it was not an illusion and at what price she gained the authentic reality. Anyone may say, "I will be a saint." But holiness must be willed wholeheartedly, with a will stronger than the might of nature and of sin, with a resolution equal to that of the grace which can bring down the "dark night" upon us for our own good. Thérèse was to know those long starless nights, but at the moment, she smiles at the sky and the sky seems to smile back. Before it opened its gates, Heaven was to crush her with all its weight of love.

Chapter Four

Thérèse at School

Of course I shall be accused of exaggerating the part of man and proportionately lessening the part of God in the formation of Thérèse. But God is behind all human actions; he suggests them or allows them and makes use even of our mistakes. I am concerned solely to get at the truth, and I put down nothing here that I do not think is true. Now, it seems to me that all the evidence points to their having set out in utter good faith to make a great saint at Les Buissonnets. With the connivance of Heaven, M. Martin deliberately tried to form the character and soul of his favorite daughter according to the pattern that seemed to him loveliest and most desirable, and he never missed an opportunity of talking about her glorious namesake, the heart-pierced Maid of Avila.

The elder girls backed him up, especially Pauline, Thérèse's "little mother," who, as I have said, was in charge of her lessons. She brought as much strictness as gentleness to her task and exacted obedience without appeal; from her Thérèse learned to overcome the little weaknesses of everyday life, absentmindedness, whims, foolish fears. "Sometimes you would send me alone after dark to fetch something from a room at the other end of the house, and would allow no refusal. That was very good for me; otherwise I should have become very timorous. It is not easy to frighten me now."

Once a thing was settled, Pauline never altered it; Thérèse had to learn to deserve, which is the A, B, C of the love of God. "Have I been a good girl today? Is dear Jesus pleased with me?" she would ask before going to sleep. And if she had to be told no, she would sob in her dark room for hours, try as she would not to shed those accusing tears. Every year there was a prize-giving, especially for her, when her father put into her quivering hands rewards exactly proportioned to her progress. It was "like a rehearsal of the Last Judgment."

Pauline listened to her confidences, resolved her doubts, explained the eternal mysteries; she was full of questions, and an answer was always forthcoming. "Why doesn't God give the same glory to all his chosen?" Pauline sent her for her silver mug, hardly bigger than a thimble, and for M. Martin's big tumbler; then she filled them both to the brim to illustrate how all the blessed receive full measure according to their capacity. Thérèse in her heart of hearts wanted to be a large vessel, but she resigned herself to her littleness and soon made a virtue of this necessity.

From his attic room, whence he could see a great distance over the tops of the trees in all directions, M. Martin arranged and directed the lifework of those committed to his care. Pauline would become a nun, and possibly Mary would follow her, Léonie was more doubtful, but Céline was promising. As for Thérèse, he felt her to be such a part of himself, so perfectly at one with him in thoughts and ideas, that he gave her as he gave himself, without suspecting that in ten years' time, when the hour had come, he would find his promise most hard to keep.

He looked forward expectantly to the visit of his "little queen" every evening and would keep her with him a long time. Up there between Heaven and earth, they talked lovingly together about the beauties of this world and the glories of that which is to come, and sometimes about the evils of the times, France, her difficulties, her future — M. Martin was not yet out of the flesh. Although he was a bit of a dreamer, after the kind of Chateaubriand or Rousseau, with something of the *Promeneur Solitaire* about him, he was nevertheless level-headed enough, a sensible solid Frenchman. The politics that he would apply to his country's affairs were drawn from the Bible; he made suggestions and proposed remedies. Thérèse was lost in admiration of his lightest word. "If you talk like that to the great men in the government, they will take you away and make you king sure enough, Papa dear. And then France will be happier than she's ever been before . . . But then I shouldn't have you to be my king all to myself. I think I'd like it better that they shouldn't know you." A lover's jealousy. Her father would smile and kiss her.

Thérèse would watch her father at prayer — a saint could not pray better — and she tells us that when there was a sermon in church, she would look at him more than at the preacher: his beautiful, sad face said so much to her. He seemed to be rapt in another world, an angel on earth — and an angel cannot die. Her love for him bordered on worship, until she was recalled to reality by a bitter warning. When she was six, she had a vision about her "darling king."

I must say in passing that phenomena of this sort were very rare in her life; there were none while she was a Carmelite, and I have found only three altogether. There had been the sprites dancing on the barrel at Alençon, and there was to be the smiling statue that would raise her cured from a sick bed. And in between, there was this ominous specter. Thérèse was not a visionary and did not expect to see Heaven opened to her every other minute. The objective value of her evidence is unusually convincing; when she says what she has seen, that *is* what she has seen, and we must believe her. I will let her tell the story herself, only emphasizing that this occurrence took place in broad daylight and when she was wide awake.

> My father was away from home and not yet expected back. It was about two or three o'clock in the afternoon of a sunny day, when everything was looking lovely. I was alone at a window opening onto the garden, my mind full of pleasant thoughts, when I saw in front of me, against the wash-house, a man dressed exactly like my father, of the same height and with the same walk, but stooping and much aged. I say aged to explain his general appearance, because I did not see his face, for his head was heavily veiled. He was moving slowly, with regular steps, along the edge of my little patch of garden. An unearthly fear came over me, and I called out loud in a trembling voice, "Father! Father!" But the uncanny person did not seem to hear, and went on without making a sign toward the clump of firs that broke the main garden path. I was waiting to see him come out on the other side of these trees, but the prophetic vision had disappeared!

Mary and Pauline, startled by the distressing cry, came running to ask why she had called their father when she knew he was not at home. Thérèse explained what she had seen, and Mary said at once that the nurse had tried to frighten her by hiding her head with her apron. Victoire was called, but she had not been out of the kitchen, and anyway she was not the sort of girl to play tricks of that kind. So they ran out into the garden and looked for the mysterious visitor, under the firs, among the bushes, in the wash-house. There was nobody to be found. Thérèse let them run about and talk; for herself, she was certain that she had seen and recognized her father, him and no one else.

The hidden meaning of that premonitory shadow will be seen later on. Meanwhile, it had bitten into Thérèse, body and soul, and the memory of it remained like an unhealing wound. It was borne in on her that her beloved father was not invulnerable; perhaps harm had already come to him. Must she give up everything and tear even him from her heart? M. Martin came back in safety from Alençon and was welcomed most joyously, but Thérèse's too-human love had henceforward taken the veil, the thick veil that covered her father's face.

Life went on. The impressionable child waited for the threatened misfortune, and none came; there were games, daydreaming, prayer, headaches, fits of crying, plenty of little trials, but happiness was unbroken. Les Buissonnets was a garden of Eden, where they loved one another and loved God. The Benedictine nuns were preparing Céline for her First Communion. On the evening before, Thérèse sat in a corner at home and listened to the further guidance given by her elder sister. From that she learned that from this great day, one must "begin a new life," and she resolved to renew hers from Céline's day.

When she was eight and a half, she began to go to school at the abbey of Notre Dame du Pré, which Léonie had just left. Céline was already in a higher class, and Thérèse could see her only from afar. She did not at all like going away from Les Buissonnets, but every evening, the maid, or more often M. Martin, fetched her back to her loved ones, her dreams, and her bed.

To reach the school, she had to go right across Lisieux — past rows of respectable middle-class houses, through the park, with its trees and terraces, that surrounds the museum (a handsome building in the style of Versailles), and past the cliff-like towers, one romanesque and one gothic, of St. Peter's cathedral in the square where M. Guérin lived; then through the narrow, picturesque, and dirty streets of timber-framed houses, with little square panes to the windows, and lastly through the working-men's quarter, in which the Benedictine convent seems to be lost. Lisieux is like a cow in a meadow, a quiet, gloomy, heavy, sleepy town, without the friendly sociable look of Alençon; it is traversed by inky rivulets and dark sordid alleys on which the factories leave a permanent deposit of thick soot, and the place comes to life, with a raucous laugh, only on market days or when a fair is on. The Thérèsian pilgrimages will bring about its modernization one day, but they will not spiritualize it or even succeed in making it quite clean; they only increase its commonplaceness: it is a show-place for tourists and a spa for the pious.

I do not think Thérèse at all liked having to plunge into the old quarters of the town, although she went only into their churches and convents. The abbey had high gray walls and was a place of bare courtyards, sickly lime trees, and nooks that hardly saw the sun. Did she like it? . . . When she entered there, she had to leave flowers and fields as well as home behind her. Did she still have at least the joys of God?

She had a companion, her cousin Mary Guérin, who was fond of her and, it seems, admired her. They were both of an age and shared the same taste for prayer and quiet. But when one is not used to it, it is difficult to be recollected in the middle of a crowd of more or less wild little girls, who, in class, do the bare minimum that will keep them out of trouble and, in playtime, go right off their heads. The common life of a school was very distressing to so rare and fastidious a spirit, shy as much from pride as from modesty. Thérèse had no idea of human society; she was a hot-house plant, sheltered from all contradiction. Here she found jealousies, rudeness, spite, disputes, in their childish guise, and into that hurly-burly she was thrown.

She was put into the green class, so called because its members wore a green ribbon for badge, and although she was the youngest, she was also the most advanced. As she worked hardest as well and was most anxious to get on — to please God and her father and herself — she was top in everything except spelling and arithmetic. "I found it very hard," she says, "to learn things word for word."

The nuns who taught never noticed this, but they soon detected the spirit of perseverance and obedience behind her gravity; they recognized a chosen soul, already used to referring all to God, and took her to their hearts. It is possible that they showed an unwise favoritism toward her, but there was no need of that to excite envy and malice against Thérèse; her success in class was a sufficient reason. A big girl of fourteen, stupid and probably plain, angry at being beaten in everything and hearing her praises always sung, stirred up the others against Thérèse and made her pay for her good looks, her charm, her hard work, and her success. It is easy to imagine the sneaking contempt, the teasing, the sneers, the nasty little lies, with which they tormented their victim; she was powerless to resist and could take refuge only in tears.

She got less fond of play, especially noisy games, and preferred reading, soaking herself in heroic or doleful tales, the life of Joan of Arc and *La Fleur du Prisonnier*. Still, she had to take some part in games or she would have been disobedient to the rules. She also turned her attention to the youngsters in the infants' class, gathering them around her to tell them the adventures of Puss-in-Boots; she was a splendid storyteller, but a mistress put a stop to this pleasure. With Mary Guérin or some other faithful friend, she would walk quietly around the playground, saying the Rosary under her breath, and sometimes she would find a dead bird and give it decent burial in some corner. Not Christian burial — Thérèse knew better than to mix up the order of nature with the order of grace in that way — but as one of God's creatures; it had been made by Him to live and be happy, and its body deserved honor as a testimony of His handiwork and His goodness.

During playtime, the children were at liberty, if they wished, to go and pray before the Blessed Sacrament in the chapel. Thérèse never missed this opportunity, and as she went through the nuns' cloister, she would kiss the pierced feet of the great crucifix on the wall. One day, she took aside one of the older pupils and asked her (much to the girl's embarrassment) to teach her how to "make a meditation." Thérèse told her that on holidays she used to hide herself in the corner between the wall and her bed, wrap one of the curtains around herself, and stop like that for a long time.

"What do you do there?" asked the elder girl.

"I think."

One of the mistresses was told the same thing and asked what she thought about.

"Why, about God, and how quickly the days go by, and eternity; *I just think*."

In spite of the kindly care of the nuns, she had to bear the burden of loneliness throughout her school days. It hurt her, and she reveled in it. Without seeking it, she served her apprenticeship under conditions that were contrary to her expansive nature but favorable to the ambition that was maturing and refining in her heart. She often played at hermits with her cousin Mary: while one tilled the ground, the other tilled her soul by prayer; and to maintain a custody of the eyes suitable to solitaries, they would walk to school with their eyes shut, hugging the fronts of the houses — they knocked over a grocer's stall or fruiterer's basket more than once. Thérèse longed for the wilderness from the bottom of her heart and discovered that Pauline had the same ambition. It seemed to her obvious that they should seek it together.

Presently she was promoted to the violet class and began to prepare for her First Communion. At catechism, she sat among inattentive companions and drank in the chaplain's words. She asked him questions, and difficult ones, too. She did not agree, for example, that children who die without Baptism enjoy only a natural happiness, without the sight of God. Why should this be so, since they have not sinned? She was desperately anxious that everybody should be saved, whether they wanted to be or not. She found free will a stumbling-block. "I wanted God to *force* everybody to be good, because he was able to." If not, then *she* would do the forcing, she, little Thérèse. Her will to power and her will to conquest had found their object.

Then one day, she heard Pauline tell Mary that she had made up her mind to enter Carmel as soon as possible. That was the wilderness that she had talked about and that Thérèse was to share with her. And now she was going to leave her behind! "In a flash, I experienced the reality of life," she writes. "I did not yet know the happiness of sacrifice . . . I was weak, just weak."

She actually thought she was going to die. Pauline comforted her and explained the cloistered life. Thérèse was at once enamored of it. She stopped crying and felt a new and strange joy filling her heart: she knew quite certainly that God was calling her, too, to Carmel. She told her sister at once, and Pauline let her carry her news to Mother Mary of Gonzaga, who was the Carmelite prioress. So it came about that Thérèse for the first time entered the house that she was so greatly to honor. She was only nine, and a postulant must be sixteen. The prioress pretended to believe in her vocation, and Thérèse began to consider what name she should adopt in religion. Her own was already taken by another, and worthily: "Thérèse of Jesus." But she was unwilling to give it up. Why not Thérèse of the Child Jesus, since she loved Him so much? Certainly that should be it. Before she left, the prioress said to her, "When you join us, dear child, you shall be called Thérèse of the Child Jesus." Such a happy coincidence of thoughts delighted her, but she had scarcely reached the street when her pleasure was dashed: "Pauline is going away. She will be lost to me!"

This devastating thought soon became an obsession. Pauline went into the convent on October 2, 1882, and Thérèse was allowed to catch an occasional glimpse of her for a few minutes in the parlor; she hated that room, with its grating and curtains. She did not eat, she did not sleep, and by the end of the year, the disconsolate child was suffering from a series of chronic headaches that put a stop to her schooling. It was the beginning of a bad breakdown, whose nature defied medical diagnosis; Thérèse, in *The Story of a Soul,* attributes it to the malevolence of the Evil One.

Was it a nervous disorder or a case of possession? The Devil is fond of making a dead-set at saints, especially when they are in embryo and relatively frail. Being unable to harm the soul directly, he wreaks his malice on body and brain; hidden powers control his victims, who break out into physical contortions and terrifying cries, uttering unintelligible nonsense; they have shocking hallucinations and eventually collapse into a deathlike prostration. That is an exact summary of Thérèse's condition. With wild eyes and disheveled hair, she got up in bed, jumped over the rail, and fell heavily to the floor without hurting herself. She was put back and had to be held down. Her bed was beset with precipices, nails in the wall were "big black burning fingers," her father's hat was some monster — then a hoarse scream and the collapse into stupor. Was it Thérèse doing these things, or was it another? She assures us that in the worst attacks, she always remained conscious of what was going on around her and that she kept the use of all her faculties. The doctor confessed that he knew neither how to treat the disorder nor how it was likely to develop.

Pauline's clothing with the Carmelite habit drew near, and this brought a few days' respite to the sufferer. She got rid of her "double" and asked that she might be taken to the ceremony. She went in a cab and was able to pray and cry and smile, to hide under her "little mother's" veil, and to nurse the hope of one day wearing it herself. But the very next day, the mysterious seizures came down on her again and more violently than ever. Her condition seemed desperate, and it was feared that if she did recover, her mind would be permanently deranged. A novena of Masses was arranged in the church of Our Lady of Victories at Paris, and her father and sisters, her uncle, aunt, and cousins, the Carmelites, and the Benedictines joined in the prayers from afar with the passionate fervor of a forlorn hope. Observe what happened.

Thérèse had been moved into her sisters' room in the front of the house, where she could see the sky and the trees and the little statue of our Lady, her feet on the serpent, stars around her head, which she had known since her earliest years; it stood on a bracket near the white curtains of the bed. The day was a Sunday, May 13, 1883, and Thérèse seemed to be sleeping. Mary and Léonie were sitting with her, and seeing that she was quiet, Mary went out of the room for a moment. Suddenly Léonie, who was reading at the window, heard Thérèse call out softly, "Mary!" She took no notice. Then Thérèse sat up and called with all her might, "Mary! Mary! Mary!" The elder girl heard her and hurried back in alarm, but when she approached the bed, Thérèse did not recognize her. Instead, she kept on calling out her name, glancing wildly about as if looking for her. This phenomenon was quite new, and the frightened Mary, after a word of instruction to Léonie, left the room to try a plan. Léonie, soothing the child as best she could, carried her to the window and showed her Mary, who was standing in the garden calling to Thérèse with outstretched arms. Thérèse could see somebody, although it was not her elder sister but some evil being that had come between them, for again she failed to recognize her. They put her back on the bed. The child was in a frightful state and aware that something extraordinary was happening. Mary and Léonie were now joined by Céline, and the three, kneeling before the image, called on our Lady with tears to intercede for their sister, who, conscious of her unhappy state but unable to explain it, added her weeping and prayers to theirs.

"All of a sudden," Thérèse tells us, "that statue came to life. Our Lady became beautiful, so beautiful that I have no words to describe her heavenly loveliness. Her face was unutterably kind and gentle, but what impressed me to my very soul was *her winning smile*. In a minute, all my sufferings were gone, and two big tears rolled down my checks." They were tears of unalloyed and heavenly joy. "Our Lady came toward me, still smiling . . . How happy I am, I thought, but I won't say so to anyone, for then my happiness would go away. Then, without any effort, I turned my eyes and saw my dear Mary; she was looking at me lovingly and seemed very moved, as though she guessed the grace I had received."

Mary had indeed seen the reflection of that divine smile in Thérèse's eyes and had a presentiment that she was healed. She was, completely healed. Within a few seconds, her malady — the malicious one, if you prefer — had gone.

Thérèse was so closely questioned by her sister that she told Mary what she had determined to tell nobody, and, as she had foreseen, her delight was soon at an end. For Mary saw fit to relate the miracle at the Carmel. Thérèse was fetched thither and, unless she was to be rude, she could not do less than try to answer the nuns' questions.

"Was she carrying the holy Child?" "Were there angels with her?" It is easy to imagine it all. The color of her gown, of her girdle, of her eyes, how she was, or was not, shod — they wanted to know everything. And as they had their own ideas on all these matters, they even anticipated the answers. Thérèse was fussed and hurt and would not say more than "Our Lady seemed to be very beautiful."

The nuns were dissatisfied. Some began to fancy that she had not looked properly or had seen wrongly, even became suspicious that she was lying or keeping something important to herself. The next thing was to decide that she was unworthy of the grace she had received; finally, to cast doubt on the vision itself.

"Our Lady allowed me to be thus tormented for my own good," she writes. "Otherwise I might have become conceited. Instead of that, I was so humiliated that I could not think of myself without extreme disgust."

She wrote this a long time after, and it may well be that she exaggerates. Nor would it be surprising if she carried away from this visit a not very favorable idea of Carmel from a human point of view. All the more reason for her to enter it . . . What is certain is that, in the end, she paid for her miraculous cure with redoubled suffering, which was now spiritual. The expression, or simply implication, of doubt about the truthfulness of her evidence revived an affliction from which she had already suffered and which was still latent, the affliction of a scrupulous conscience. Clouds closed over our Lady's smiling face, and they opened only twice again during the rest of Thérèse's earthly life.

Chapter Five

Scruples and Vocation

There could be no question of sending Thérèse back to school at once after this serious warning. She must have a long rest and plenty of diversion; there was indeed a tendency to overdo it. Several old friends invited M. Martin to stay with them near Alençon. He hated "the world" but was very fond of traveling about, and he would not deny his daughter this opportunity of sharing his pleasure. She went to country houses at Saint-Denis, at Grogny, perhaps at Lanchal, where she entered into society, wore fine clothes, and mixed with fashionably dressed ladies; she listened to their gossip and flatteries and was much petted and admired. All these luxuries and conveniences, grand rooms, expensive food, well-kept-up gardens, crowds of smart servants were enough to turn the head of a child who was only just enjoying sunlight and peace — and in her beloved native country — after emerging from an atrocious nightmare. If she had been willing to give herself up to it, she could, in time, have become a leader in this elegant and futile world. All these people were serving God, or thought they were (without ever giving up a single one of their pleasures), and yet no one ever seemed to think about death; that was what puzzled Thérèse. And probably it was this consideration that kept her from slipping down the path of easygoing enjoyment. "All earthly things are vanity," she declared in after-years when she remembered these enchanting days.

She had not forgotten that our Lord was waiting for her, over a year already, at his altar and, on her return, took up her preparation with increased fervor, first at home and then at school. Mary now took over the instruction that had formerly been given by Pauline. Pauline sent Thérèse an album in which she could keep a record of her "good deeds" in an exclusively "poetical" form: to each act of love or self-denial there was a corresponding floweret: daisy, cornflower, violet, rose, forget-me-not. It is a tradition (quite a hundred years old!) of the Carmelite and some other orders to clothe the most serious ideas and the most vigorous actions with a garment of pretty-prettiness, and the young nun sought to instill this practice into her sister. It was confirmed by much that she saw and heard among the Benedictine nuns (for neither were they averse from flowers), and Thérèse received an indelible impress. The fact must be accepted. To these worthy nuns, what was not sentimental was not nice, and what was not nice could be neither beautiful nor religious. We have seen beneath this veil, and we know that in Thérèse it sheltered solid determination and energy.

Mary was not so keen on this sort of thing. She was less imaginative and artistic than Pauline and did not put so much sugar into her guidance and advice. Thérèse had rather misunderstood her eldest sister but now became greatly attached to her, for all that some of her inclinations were sharply curbed. Mary was suspicious of "meditation," fearing the child would lose herself in daydreams, and allowed her to make only vocal, "set" prayers.

The secret of the smiling Madonna had been well kept by the Carmelites, so nothing was known about it at the abbey, where

Thérèse made her retreat before First Communion. She always remembered this as a blessed time. Every night, the sister directress came to the dormitory with her little lamp, drew aside the bed curtains, and kissed her.

There is no need to describe the child's feelings when at last, pale and trembling and in a dress like flakes of snow, she walked up the nuns' chapel to the high, dark screen dividing the nave from the choir. It was a superb setting for this first embrace with God: austere, very *grand siècle*, a little jansenistic.

"Thérèse looked more like an angel than a human being," said the prioress. She was crying at the altar, much to the surprise of her fellows, who supposed that she had some qualm of conscience or was missing her dead mother or the absent Pauline. They knew nothing about weeping for joy. A deep and unutterable happiness had in fact swept across her and overflowed from her eyes.

"O my God, I love You. I am Yours forever." That was all she could think and all she could say. She asked nothing of her Lord, he asked nothing of her; there was a reciprocal gift, without conditions. It was more than a kiss, she said; it was a making-one. The drop of water was absorbed in the limitless ocean: Thérèse surrendered her own will and joined her weakness to the almightiness of her King.

The new communicant went to visit the novice Pauline, and the day ended with a family party at Les Buissonnets. She was given a watch for a present. It did not seem to her the most important thing.

The Bread of Life brings hunger at the same time that it nourishes. Thérèse made her second Communion, with her father and Mary, on Ascension Day, but afterward had to wait a long time, until other big feasts came around, and the time went very slowly.

Confirmation, on the following Whitsunday,[4] brought her a new grace, the strength to suffer, and she was soon to be in need of it.

Soon after, she had an example of human fickleness and unreliability. A friend of whom she was very fond went away for a time, and her return was looked forward to with quivering excitement. When she came back, she had forgotten Thérèse and hardly looked at her. Thérèse tried to work off her abounding affection on this or the other of the nuns at school, but they did not lend themselves to it and, indeed, did not seem to understand what she wanted. It is hardly to be expected that they should, for reserve and diffidence paralyzed her tongue before it could give any hint. So she continued to be lonely. This was a good thing on the whole, for it probably saved her from worse disappointments, and she already had enough ties to break without adding to them.

She was approaching the anniversary of her First Communion when scrupulosity, which had been troubling her imperceptibly, became disturbingly apparent. The attack lasted for nearly two years.

The sinner has no scruples because he has no conscience, or else because he has trained it not to be upset by anything. Scrupulosity always indicates a desire for perfection, even when it bewilders and leads astray. It is a sort of hypersensitiveness of the conscience that ferrets out the byways of the soul; it probes into actions and motives, analyzes them, isolates them, lays bare what it finds — and then what it does not. It leads to a chronic shortsightedness which makes everything doubtful and suspicious, so that there is no certainty even of a good intention. From being unable to judge, the scrupulous person becomes unable to act and wears himself out with self-torment and self-reproach. Unless he

[4] Pentecost.

can get over it — and abandonment of oneself to God will restore sanity — he is done for: despair and suicide lie in wait for him. This form of mental alienation is always a hell for the victim of it in its acute stage; but it may also lead to a complete purification of mind and will and affections, even to the degree where God thinks, wills, and loves through his creature.

Thérèse was now nearly twelve, and from the day when she was first able to grasp the idea of cause and effect, she had learned to value the least of her thoughts, words, and deeds in terms of worth and worthlessness; by constant practice, she had become more and more skillful and sharp in the discernment of the real motives behind her actions.

Of course, she had a confessor, but children of her age do not have a special director, and she referred her difficulties to Mary, in default of Pauline, who might have understood them better. But could Mary be relied on? Thérèse reached the stage of doubting others as much as herself. It was useless for grown-up people to try to reassure her, for whenever she examined her conscience — and she was always examining it — her every deed seemed sinful.

During the holidays, her aunt took her to the seaside for a fortnight. Wasn't it rather frivolous to amuse herself with donkey-rides and shrimping? She was given a pretty blue ribbon. Ought she to take it? Ought she to tie up her hair with it? Ought she to look in the glass and think that it suited her? But all the girls were wearing blue bows. All the worse, for perhaps they ought not to. She would have refused it, but that would have been unkind to her aunt. Moreover, to refuse it might be a sin of pride, an affectation of simplicity, an arrogation of moral superiority to all the other little girls. But what if it *was* wrong to wear it, after all? What was the truth about it all?

When she had not scruples of her own, they were gratuitously suggested to her. She often had headaches, but as she never complained, nobody pitied her. Her cousin Mary had them, too, but she made a fuss and was coddled accordingly. "Why don't you do the same?" Thérèse asked herself.

"No, my child, you're shamming. That won't do." This is harmless enough, but the humiliated and mortified child judged herself to be always wrong and probably ended by believing that she hadn't a headache at all. The result can be guessed.

It was even worse at school, where association with others raised so many delicate problems. Thérèse could never get out of her mind the painted pin-box, which she had seen in the hands of a companion, who had given it to her to please her. If she had not shown so much admiration for that little box, her friend would not have been deprived of it; she had taken advantage of her kindness. But wouldn't it offend her generosity and make things worse to give it back? . . .

These apparent trifles wrung Thérèse's soul. Ordinarily they ended in tears, but soon she would be reproaching herself for them: to whatever sin she had committed, she was now adding that of weakness; she must be more brave. In the end, she was crying for having cried. Her work suffered by all this; so did her health, and even her prayers. M. Martin took her away from school, but being at home did not effect a cure; she pestered Mary with childish and insoluble "cases of conscience." As she grew up, she became more and more pretty; people were not slow to tell her so, and she was annoyed with herself at knowing it. But she saw herself already sunk in profligacy — if she knew what the word meant. "What should I have become," she asks later on, "if the world had smiled on me from my birth . . . if my heart had not been so soon turned toward God?" Mary did her best to comfort her, but the next minute, Thérèse would fall back into an agony of uncertainty.

She used to go to her former school to take part in the meetings of the Children of Mary sodality. "I would work away quietly at my allotted task, and then, when I had finished and nobody was taking any notice, I would slip into the gallery of the chapel and stop there till my father came to fetch me. It was there that I found my only consolation; wasn't Jesus my best friend? I could talk happily only to him: my spirit was oppressed by conversation with people, even about religious things." To talk alone with God was her saving refuge.

At this period of her life, she seems, whether out of shy respect or for fear of troubling him, to have been reticent with M. Martin about her interior trials. When, therefore, Mary also went into Carmel and Thérèse accordingly lost her only confidante, she turned toward the innocent souls of the little brothers and sisters who died before her birth. Surely, she thought, those who are living in peace and happiness before the throne of God, who never came even within the shadow of the wings of the Prince of this world, must pity her distress and be able to enlighten and relieve her.

An answer came on the night of Christmas 1886: the newly born Babe of babes, without utterance or showing of Himself, changed her darkness into "torrents of brightest light"; He who was made weak that she might be made strong gave her back her weapons of love. As usual, she had put out her shoes in the hearth (doubtless she had no illusions about this proceeding, but it was very nice to have presents and surprises, whether they were brought by little Jesus or by her father and sisters). When she came back from midnight Mass, she overheard her father say, "This is much too childish for a big girl like Thérèse. This will be the last time." The apparent reproach might have upset her grievously, but in fact her heart was changed. She kept back her tears and was unaffectedly pleased with the presents that she found in her shoes; her simplicity of outlook had come back, and henceforward she was able to get the better of her sensitiveness and scruples. "The source of my tears dried up and afterward flowed only occasionally and with difficulty." She had learned from the Child in the manger that all her troubles arose from self-sufficiency and self-esteem, from a vainglorious concern about her own reactions and the inordinate value that she put on herself. What God actually asked from her was simply goodwill. She had to forget herself and carry his care and love to others. "Charity came into my heart . . . and from then on I was happy." We shall see for how long.

One day, a card slipped partly from her missal, disclosing a single nail-pierced hand of the crucified Savior. That precious blood runs down to the earth, and nobody comes forward to gather it up; who will stand by the Cross to receive the life-giving stream and pour it out upon the multitudes? "I will," said Thérèse. "That is my vocation." Her Well-beloved thirsted, and the more He emptied Himself, the greater was His thirst; He shed His Blood only that we might thirst and be filled, until our souls are running over and He, too, may drink thereat. A longing to drink at this fountain had taken hold of Thérèse, to drink and to enable others to, a longing to wind all around the world that river of grace that flows from the divine side and must return to it. It is impossible to think of oneself when one is drowning in the Blood of God.

At fourteen, Thérèse had left the frontier state of childhood and reached a balanced condition of reason stayed by faith. She knew that work is an indefeasible duty, but she never cared for household jobs and was always dispensed from them, being looked upon as something special, marked for a very high destiny. She would not refuse to help her sisters, but was eaten up with a greed for learning that absorbed all the time she did not give to prayer. She was given formal lessons by a lady in the town and added to them "special branches of knowledge" that she studied by herself. She had "poetical" sensibility and appreciation of beautiful things but did not cultivate any "accomplishments"; this was as well, for when people of her social class adventure among the arts, they rarely escape the accepted "idealism" of the *bourgeoisie*.

In a spirit of self-denial, Thérèse had refused to learn drawing. She took it up only in the cloister, "taught by the Holy Ghost," as some biographers assert. In my opinion, it is better not thus to commit the Spirit of God, and I shall confine myself to a consideration of the intention of her later pictures (as of Pauline's and Céline's). Her religious understanding developed and deepened. Her bedside book was the *Imitation*,[5] probably the only one that was any good to her, and she knew it almost by heart. She tells us that a modern work about "the end of this world and the mysteries of the future life"[6] enabled her "to add plenty of honey and oil to the pure flour."

When Céline left school, she again became Thérèse's constant companion, her confidante, and the "sister of her soul." They would go up into the attic-room in the evening and together try to learn the secrets of the kingdom behind the stars. "It seems to me that we were given great graces." There is no doubt that the chief one was the regular practice of charity and renouncement. And the more she gave, the more she had, according with the word of the Gospel: "For he that hath, to him shall be given, and he shall abound." She did not even ask her confessor to allow her to make

[5] St. Thomas à Kempis's *Imitation of Christ*.

[6] See Father Charles Arminjon, *The End of the Present World and the Mysteries of the Future Life*, trans. Susan Conroy and Peter McEnerny (Manchester, New Hampshire: Sophia Institute Press, 2008).

more frequent Communions. But God prompted him to suggest it himself, even to the extent of several times a week, and her cup of happiness was filled.

But the call of the wilderness, of Carmel, was every day clearer and more insistent. The only person who gave her any encouragement in this connection was Pauline. She had now been a nun for five years and had exchanged the white veil of the novice for the black of the professed; she had tasted the hardships and the solaces of the religious life, and was clearsighted enough to be reasonably sure of the reality of her sister's vocation. Mary would not hear of it, and Céline knew nothing about it — she would have been jealous at the suggestion of a younger sister preceding her into a convent. As for M. Martin, Thérèse realized what a blow it would be for him and put off indefinitely the bad moment when she would have to tell him.

Moreover, he had just recovered from a first stroke of paralysis and had to be carefully looked after. Meanwhile, time was getting on. Thérèse had fixed on the following Christmas as the latest date for her entry into religion, ten days before the fifteenth anniversary of her birth. She had said, "I wish it," and it must be.

On Whitsunday, she was given some of that flaming courage that came down upon the Apostles in the upper room. She besought God to impart it also to her father, and after Vespers, she went to look for him. He was sitting in the garden behind the house, at the spot now spoiled by that frightful commemorative monument. It was a lovely day, promising a long mild evening; the cycle of the liturgical year was once more accomplished and the promise kept: *I will ask the Father, and He shall give you another Comforter, the Spirit of truth.*[7] There was now naught to do but to worship and to

[7] John 14:16.

join oneself to the fullness of the Spirit. Thérèse approached, her eyes full of tears and her heart of resolution, and sat down on the seat beside her father. He looked at her, drew her head tenderly down on to his shoulder, and asked her gently, "What is it, my little queen?"

As he got no answer, he rose to his feet and, with his arm still about her, led her slowly among the trees. Then Thérèse told him everything, simply and in detail: the fruit of grace was ripe. M. Martin burst into tears, but he did not protest, and the only objection he put forward was that she was still very young to make so serious a decision. This was not difficult to overcome, for he had himself waited and wished for this consummation. He pulled himself together and spoke to her like the good man he was. Picking a tiny lily-like flower from the wall, he gazed at it, considering the care with which God had made it take root and thrive there; yet it could go on growing, perhaps even better, in another soil, for its roots were not severed. That flower was a figure of his daughter, whom he must uproot from his heart and replant in the garden of God.

M. Martin having acquiesced, so did the prioress of the Carmel. When Uncle Guérin was consulted, he took his stand on human prudence; he was listened to with respect and the cogency of his arguments admitted. From being at the gate of paradise, Thérèse found herself in the garden of affliction. Her agonized uncertainty lasted for three days, and then M. Guérin, quite spontaneously, changed his mind and agreed with his brother-in-law; he, too, was a good man. It remained only to approach the authorities. But the ecclesiastical superior of the Carmelites, Canon Delatroette, declared at once and most definitely that no girl could join them until she had completed her twenty-first year, unless she had a dispensation from the bishop. This was the biggest blow as yet, and a difficulty that nobody had foreseen.

A Thérèse Martin is not easily discouraged; her stubborn nature was positively immovable when she had God on her side. She would go and see the bishop; if he gave her no satisfaction, she would go to the Pope; if he was not acquiescent, then God would make him yield: that was her attitude. God wanted what she wanted, and he would have the last word.

Meanwhile, she doubled her prayers, her self-deprivations, and her almsdeeds: the time when she would take refuge in tears had gone by, and the picture of her as a little weeping flower was never more false than it was now. She went to church, and she visited the needy. When a poor mother was taken ill, she looked after her small children and taught them their catechism; she took an endless delight in imprinting her spirit on their docile souls, and her mark was ineffaceable. And then there were the souls of sinners — but how could she reach them, and had she any power over them? Would they be lost in that pit from which no act of love ever rises? She wanted God to be loved even in hell, and for that end, she would go down into it. When someone asked her, "What is a soul?" she answered without the slightest hesitation that it is "a spiritual being created *solely* to love God."

Newspapers were hardly ever read at Les Buissonnets, for they are full of nasty things that should be of no interest to Christian girls. But M. Martin took in *La Croix*, from which he kept his daughters informed of passing events. During that summer of 1887, "the crime in the rue Montaigne" was agitating public opinion. A low adventurer called Pranzini, receiver, thief, and pimp, had murdered a well-known courtesan, together with her maid and the maid's little girl, and had been arrested at Marseilles when trying to dispose of the woman's jewelry. There was no redeeming feature about this man or his life: he was a barefaced and bestial ruffian, but a handsome ruffian, with an infinite capacity for seduction — hence, the interest taken in him by the world in general and women in particular. He protested his innocence but was found guilty and condemned to death, a penalty that he deserved even had he killed nobody. His callousness suggested that he was certainly a lost soul. That soul Thérèse coveted. How and why, God alone knows. She knew nothing about him except his crime, his stubborn impenitence, and his threatened fate, but among so many sinful souls, she chose the one that seemed the worst and most hideous to implore God's mercy for it. This was the first that she reclaimed, using every spiritual means imaginable; herself, all the resources of the Church, and the boundless merits of Jesus Christ were offered for Pranzini's ransom.

> I felt certain within myself that I should be heard, but to get courage to go on with my attempted conquest of souls I made this prayer: O my God, I am sure You will forgive this unhappy Pranzini, and I have such trust in Your infinite mercy that I shall still be sure even if he does not ask for a priest or show any sign of repentance. But this is my first sinner, and because of that, I ask You for a *sign* of his salvation to encourage me!

On the day after the execution, she could not refrain from opening her father's newspaper, hoping to find in it the sign she had asked. She read that at the very moment when the wretched man, unrepentant, unshriven, unabsolved, was led beneath the guillotine, he had pushed the executioners aside, seized the crucifix from the chaplain's hands, and kissed the sacred wounds several times.

Thérèse slipped away to hide her tears; she had a right to cry. When we consider the filthy lips of her "first child" (that is what she called the criminal) we can feel no surprise at the numberless conversions that she has obtained and still obtains; but in this crusade for souls, her first victory remains unsurpassed.

In spite of her apparent excitement when the time came, it was a mere nothing for the saver of Pranzini's soul to present herself before a bishop to ask for a dispensation. She went to Bayeux for this purpose on October 31. So that she should look less young, she put up her hair for the first time and wore a saucy little hat with two white feathers: it was not easy to recognize the schoolgirl with dainty features framed in a cloud of gold. Now her hair was drawn back *en chignon*, her face was seen to be clear-cut and strongly marked, her expression determined, almost brutally frank, and of a baffling guilelessness: a face such as painters give to Joan of Arc and the great Teresa. She wept before the bishop, but spoke up plainly and fearlessly, keeping back nothing of what she had meant to say. She made so strong an impression that instead of discouraging her, he counseled patience; her father had made up his mind to take her to Rome, and that visit would strengthen her vocation. The bishop furthermore promised that he would himself take the matter up with the chaplain of the Carmelites at Lisieux and would let her father know the result of his efforts. M. Martin showed himself as anxious to give his daughter as she was to give herself.

Three days later, she set out for Rome, together with her father and Céline and a party of rather aristocratic pilgrims. Her piercing insight soon detected the spiritual insufficiency that lurked behind some of these high titles and great names and certain of the cassocks. This last discovery perplexed her; she had not as yet realized why the reformed Carmelites had been appointed, as their first duty, to pray for the clergy. It was a sad disillusionment. If the best among them were so ineffectual, what could be said of the rest? There could not be a more noble work than to bring back enthusiasm to the lukewarm and to lead on the ardent to yet greater efforts, to be a custodian of the savor of the salt of the earth.

They visited Paris, and at Our Lady of Victories Thérèse received strong interior confirmation of the smile whereby she had been healed four years before; on Montmartre she consecrated herself to the Sacred Heart. As might be expected, she admired the monuments in the cemetery at Milan, realistic lachrymose sculptures of the most disagreeable kind set up by the wealthy in memory of their dead. At Venice, she was struck by the melancholy of the place; at Padua, she venerated the Franciscan Antony; at Bologna, the Franciscan Catherine; at Loreto, the Holy House. Loreto pleased her especially, and she received Holy Communion there. At Rome, she risked her neck to kiss the blood-soaked earth of the Colosseum (it was not so accessible then as it is now); she lay down beside Céline in the empty resting-place of St. Cecilia in the catacomb of Callistus, visited her house under the church in the Trastevere, and acquired a deep devotion to her; from the basilica of St. Agnes she brought away a tessera of mosaic for Pauline (now Sister Agnes of Jesus). Eventually she found herself at the feet of Pope Leo XIII.

The vicar general of Bayeux, M. Révérony, who had accompanied the pilgrims and had his eye on Thérèse from the start, was standing beside the Pope, having warned the people that they must not speak to him. Thérèse spoke.

"Most holy father," she said, raising tear-filled eyes to his, "I have a great favor to ask you."

Getting no reply, she went on: "In honor of your jubilee, let me go into Carmel when I'm fifteen."

"The superiors have the matter in hand, your holiness," interposed the vicar general.

"Very well," said Leo. "Do as the superiors decide."

But Thérèse tried again. "If only you say yes, holy father, nobody will raise any difficulty."

Surprised and moved, the Pope looked searchingly at her and answered impressively, "You will enter if it is God's will."

Then two attendants raised her from her knees, and Leo stretched out his hand to her lips. Thérèse went out sick with grief, but deep in her heart there was the peace that comes from a good conscience.

She tells us that before leaving Rome, she offered herself to the Child Jesus to be his "little toy." There was still much of the child in her, and her ingenuous offering was surely accepted.

Chapter Six

First Trials in Carmel

From Rome, they went to Naples, then to Assisi, and back home by Florence, Pisa, and Genoa, staying all the time at the best hotels. Thérèse was enchanted by all that she saw and was continually trying to free herself from the delight of the eyes. She was suffering but, with superb obstinacy, refused to give in and went on willing her consolation — namely, the certitude that she would go into the convent at Christmas. As a distraction or to gain time, M. Martin suggested a pilgrimage to the holy places. But that would have been only a poor makeshift: the door she wanted to open, and at once, led to a Jerusalem "which is above."

When they got back to Lisieux, Thérèse, on the advice of Pauline, wrote to the bishop. The superior of the Carmelites was still against her, and the prioress for her. Better still, she had succeeded in winning over the vicar general during the pilgrimage, and he now supported her with all the means at his command.

Decidedly, she thought, God is on my side; the thing is as good as settled; and she anxiously watched the post. But God seemed to be in no hurry; he kept her on tenterhooks, doubtless thinking it well to test such assurance to the utmost. Christmas came, and still there was not a word. As usual, Thérèse went to the midnight Mass at St. Peter's cathedral — sad, perhaps a bit put out and reproachful of the holy Child. Three days later, on the feast of the Innocents, she had a letter from Mother Mary of Gonzaga.

The bishop had yielded and left the decision to the discretion of the prioress. She had only to say the word, and Thérèse might enter Carmel tomorrow . . . But the prioress thought, not at once: Lent would soon be here, and she feared what might be the effect of its special hardships on a young postulant; no matter if she were mistaken, another three months' patient waiting would do no harm. So Thérèse would be received in April, on the day on which the feast of the Annunciation was to be kept that year.

There might have been a certain danger in this further delay. "What is three months now? She will have the whole of her life to practice penance in the convent. Let her have some fun and collect as many happy memories as she can to take in with her." Just so do we hear of some prospective bridegrooms "making hay while the sun shines." Whoever whispered such an idea into Thérèse's ear underestimated the strength both of divine grace and of her own spirit. The bride of Christ was not going to lose a minute from preparing herself for service in the austere cell that is the anteroom of the bride-chamber; it was fitting that she should enter it garbed in penitence and charity rather than in human joys and regrets. Day by day and hour by hour, she spent her last "holiday" breaking what was left of her own will into little pieces. She thwarted the least slackness and the tiniest whim; she looked away when her eyes fell upon things that were dear; she forbade herself all argument and answering back; she was always at hand unostentatiously to do any little thing for people and acted at once on the least hint of what anyone wanted; in fact, she made herself the perfect servant.

First Trials in Carmel

On the evening of April 8, 1888, the family at Les Buissonnets assembled in the dining room which I have described. The chandeliers lit up the table, and it was spread with plenty of food, as befits a great festival in the house of a well-to-do *bourgeois*, even if he is a saint. But that food was only nibbled, for they were celebrating Thérèse's departure for Carmel. M. Martin was freely willing to give her up; she was experiencing the sweetest moment of her life. That does not mean that she was not deeply moved by human sadness; it would have been monstrous otherwise.

Next morning Thérèse looked smilingly upon the furniture in the house and the trees in the garden for the last time, went down the graveled path in the front, and made her way to the convent chapel, past the old church of St. James, and by the narrow dingy rue de Livarot, which crosses the Orbiquet over a little bridge. Her relatives followed her in, and they all assisted at Mass together; at the Communion, Thérèse heard sobbing all around her: she was the only one who did not cry.

But the pounding of her heart nearly stilled her when she moved toward the enclosure door. She kissed them all, knelt to receive her father's blessing, and walked in without a backward glance. The door was shut upon her, and she was embraced by the prioress, by her two sisters in the flesh and in religion, and by all her new sisters.

The formidable superior, M. Delatroette, was there, and undeterred by any fear of discord, he said sharply and loud enough for M. Martin to hear, "Well, reverend mothers, now you can sing your *Te Deum*. As delegate of his lordship the bishop, I hand over to you this fifteen-year-old child in accordance with your wish. I hope she will not disappoint your hopes; but I would remind you that if she does, the responsibility is yours." His tact was as meager as his perspicacity.

The fifteen-year-old child went quietly and resolutely to her cell; there was, as it were, a sort of majesty joined to her modesty which at once called forth the respect of her sisters.

❦

The Carmel of Lisieux stands beside a dark rivulet. It is surrounded by high walls, and a cloister runs around the tiny garden; in the middle is a large cross. The house itself is built of gloomy brick, roofed with slate, and has dormer windows and arched doors; it is icily plain and is even more leafless than the school at the abbey. The inside is made up chiefly of straight whitewashed passages and cold cells, bare of ornament except for the reminders in black-painted letters above the doors: "Watch and pray"; "To suffer and to die." From the prioress's table at the top of the refectory, the eye-sockets of a skull observe the nuns as they eat. From their choir they get a faraway view of the altar and its tabernacle through the closely set bars of a double grille, and in the parlor, the shadow and the voice of friends are occasionally discerned. Such was the paradise that Sister Thérèse had chosen.

"Everything in the convent seemed to me delightful," she writes. Her long dreamed-of wilderness was realized to perfection by the nine-foot-square cell with its single window; it was furnished with a straw mattress on a bed of boards, a jug and basin, a stool, a table, and a plain wooden cross. "Now I am here for always," she said over and over to herself. With God; far from the meanness and weakness and temptations of the world; among the perfect. This last was an illusion of which she would be cured. Wherever there is humankind, there is the world; a convent is a part of the world. God has arranged it like that.

A postulant's dress is not becoming: a skimpy black gown and bonnet have neither the dignity of a nun's habit nor the pleasant homeliness of a lay-sister's clothes. However, it is not meant to be attractive, but rather to be a test and a discouragement to any romanticism that may be lurking in the vocation. The postulant finds herself the poor relation of a not very large family (a Carmelite community rarely numbers more than twenty), every member of which has her own duties, assigned and supervised by the prioress, who is charged with the maintenance of the Carmelite rule. She has surrendered all liberty of speech, of action, of use of time: she is free only to obey.

The day, from 5 a.m. to 10:30 p.m., is divided between psalmody in choir (the whole Divine Office, unabridged), Mass, conferences on the rule, study of Latin and the Holy Scriptures, reading in common, manual work, dinner and supper, meditation, and private prayer. Everything is done in silence, that is, without a sentence or even a word that is not required by the circumstances or in reply to a question. Twice a day, a recreation of one hour's duration allows this observance to be relaxed.

These recreations are presided over by the prioress (or novice-mistress, her delegate among the junior sisters), so that order may be kept and charity maintained among the varied characters and dispositions whose welfare has been entrusted to her; she has indeed to be a mother, combining love and strictness. But as a prioress has her own personal temperament and idiosyncrasies (only the greatest saints are entirely delivered from the domination of these), she is still liable to error, imprudence, and even injustice; she is a human being, and so are her daughters. Accordingly, the thorny and humanly insoluble problem of family life and human relations is present in a convent as much as anywhere else. Natural incompatibilities, misunderstandings, conflict of personalities or policies are necessarily there in a latent state; they are concealed by the daily discipline, modified by the force of brotherly love, but they are there and often strengthened and exasperated by the unescapable propinquity of one to another. For the stronger souls, they are a source of further strength and improvement.

❧

The ladies of Lisieux discussed the latest news.

"Fancy that little Martin girl burying herself like that at her age! I'm sure she won't stop. You see!"

"Do you think not? She's very headstrong and far too proud ever to admit that she was mistaken about her vocation. She'll have a bad time, but she'll stop. They always stop there for pride — not because they want to."

Mme. X is better informed, and puts her oar in: "People take their pleasure where they find it. Believe me, these Carmelites don't have a bad time. To start off with, they've got nothing to worry about; everything is arranged for them beforehand. You go back to your childhood and let yourself be led, and it takes very little to please you."

"Aren't they always praying then?"

"Of course not. Between the services they chatter and amuse themselves, and the better-class girls do things: you know, watercolors and poetry and all that. Why, on feast-days, they have plays."

"Plays?"

"Yes, indeed. My cousin Marguerite told me so. These good nuns wanted a pet so they've taken Thérèse, and they'll make a plaything of her. Don't forget they've already got the two elder ones, and you can guess whether they're spoiled or not!"

Their minds being thus set at rest, the ladies began to coo. Were it not for their imperative duties to society, they would all go off and join Thérèse Martin.

First Trials in Carmel

The reality was very different. Not as regards enjoyments, for it is true enough that the Carmelites amused themselves with a childlike zest at recreation and on feast-days — nuns are nothing if not human. But if it had occurred to one of those "good nuns" to pet the fifteen-year-old postulant, the mature gravity of her expression would have been sufficient warning not to try. On the other hand, Thérèse should have been able to count on a certain tenderness on the part of the prioress who had helped her so kindly in difficulties besetting her vocation. But the time of trials was not over, and what Thérèse had suffered hitherto was only the beginning of what was in store for her. When she entered the convent door, she lost the privileges that had been hers outside, and the prioress made her see this plainly enough.

Mother Mary of Gonzaga was fifty-four years old and had been governing the community for two years. She belonged to a good family of the provincial nobility, which made her a little unapproachable, but she was lacking in neither kindness nor charm; she was an energetic, enterprising woman, somewhat tactless, subject to fits of depression, and, according to Msgr. Laveille, rather inconsistent. She had sudden moods and would change her mind at a moment's notice, but was nevertheless so sure of herself that she expected to be followed exactly. It can hardly be supposed that she lost all her sympathy for Thérèse directly she came into the convent; it is more likely that she reasoned somewhat in this fashion: Here is a girl who has never been outside her home, the youngest of the family and much coddled. She has been about a bit, certainly, but only with decent people among whom life was easy and everything corresponded to her wishes and often to her fads. She believes that she has been favored with special graces and even a vision. She is strong-willed, so she won't be easy to deal with. She has put her pride and ambition into the hands of God; that means that she has still got them. In spite of her desire for perfection, she imagines that everything will make way for her and all will be plain sailing because she has two sisters here. She has got to learn that that isn't so, and the kindest thing to do is to teach her.

And so poor Thérèse met the unmoved and severe expression of a superioress instead of the smiling motherly face that she had expected. It is quite likely that the postulant's clumsiness in her work about the house was irritating and that her immoderate anxiety to remedy the least fault aggravated rather than pleased the prioress. I must emphasize that she was capricious and authoritarian, although otherwise a very good woman.

The new ordeal began with coldness and went on to rebukes. Thérèse is very reserved about the persecutions, real or imaginary, that she underwent, but she narrates something of those which she declares were far from being the most cruel and tells us shyly that the mother prioress "gave it to her" every time they met. Thus: Thérèse, broom in hand, had just finished sweeping out the cloisters but had overlooked a cobweb in a dark corner. Naturally this was the first thing that the prioress saw. Her sharp voice drew everybody's attention.

"It is easy enough to see that our cloisters are swept by a child of fifteen! It's shameful!" Thérèse wished the floor would open and swallow her. "Sweep away that cobweb, and be more careful in future!"

The situation was complicated by the fact that the prioress took no notice of orders that had previously been given by the novice-mistress, who was Thérèse's immediate superior, so she did not know whom to obey. During her novitiate — a year later, her ordeal was long — the novice-mistress would send her into the garden to gather vegetables. She obeyed, trembling, for it always happened that she met the prioress, who would exclaim, "This child does absolutely nothing! What is a novice that she should be sent for a walk every day?"

"And she used to be the same with me about everything," adds Sister Thérèse. "On the rare occasions when I was with her for an hour on end, I was scolded nearly the whole time . . . and the worst of it was I did not understand how I was to correct my shortcomings."

These shortcomings were supposed to be principally "slowness" and "inattention during Divine Office." Doubtless Thérèse was thinking or meditating or simply dreaming. While the minds of the other younger sisters were concentrated on their work, hers was wandering about or thinking of something else. Too much imagination . . . or perhaps too much prayer. A time came when the prioress had to admit that the misery that her severity caused to Thérèse had never turned her aside from perfect obedience. It must have cost her something!

The novice-mistress, Mother Mary of the Angels, was a cross of another kind. She had known Thérèse from childhood and was very fond of her and, when given charge of her, continued to show it. She at once recognized a continual correspondence with grace on the part of the new postulant and took great care of her. But she talked too much, while Thérèse loved silence and cultivated it so that she might try to talk with God. This never occurred to Mother Mary, and she overwhelmed her with monotonous homilies and dreary explanations. Thérèse came almost to prefer the admonitions of the prioress. Nevertheless, carefully avoiding any criticism, she spoke to Mother Mary of all her troubles. The latter was warmly sympathetic, and to make up, imposed certain relaxations of the rule, the opportuneness of some of which Thérèse might well have questioned, while of others she certainly felt the need. For example, it was a good thing that she should be excused from Matins, for she was not getting enough sleep. But it was an excessive kindness when this relaxation was suddenly, without any special reason, prolonged for a whole fortnight. "This young lady is making herself soft!" thought the prioress. It was a pity she did not keep the thought to herself; instead, even the consideration she received was made to recoil onto Thérèse's head.

From time to time, the junior sisters would visit Mother Genevieve of St. Thérèse, a former prioress, whose infirmities kept her to her cell and often to her bed. She was a holy woman, who had attained a high order of prayer and is said to have received the gift of prophecy on more than one occasion. It is to be expected, then, that she would have seen into Thérèse's soul and divined her remarkable future. But it was hidden even from her. She did no more than encourage her, not without being sometimes startled by Thérèse's spiritual audacity and moved to put a damper on a love that seemed to flame too high. At the only opportunities that Thérèse had of going confidently to a nun who was reputed a saint, her trust was ignored, repulsed, or frozen up.

What about her sisters? They both loved her dearly, but Thérèse had not left friends outside only to recover yet closer friends in the convent. It seemed to her that natural affection, and especially family affection, ought in the cloister to give way entirely to the mutual and equal love of all the nuns in God. And she did not merely resign herself to this view; she rose above it. She was aware of the truly spiritual quality — although perhaps a little too mixed with the human — of the joy that she would have gotten from frequent association with her eldest sister and godmother, Sister Mary of the Sacred Heart, and with her "little mother," Sister Agnes of Jesus, had the mother prioress permitted it; and she had no doubt of the efficacy of the help that their tenderness and experience never failed to suggest to her. When she had been snubbed, wounded in her pride or, worse, in her good will, she longed to run to them and escape from this onslaught of pain, pain about which she must keep silence because no one was willfully responsible for it.

But by an almost superhuman act of will, she refused this most natural outlet to her feelings and made it a rule never to seek the company of her sisters on any pretext. If one of them was not well, she would even wait until someone else had been before she went to see her. "At recreation, she used to sit down by whoever was nearest her, unless she noticed anyone who had not a companion." Mary and Pauline had not yet reached their sister's degree of self-abnegation, and it may be that they thought her egoistic and ungrateful. Her deliberate reserve did not conduce to understanding, and some involuntary coolness was the result. But they understood her in the end.

So Thérèse kept her troubles to herself, there being no one to give her enlightened advice or competent direction. When it came to choosing a director, all her confessors failed her, whether from insufficiency or lack of understanding. The chaplain of the convent, Father Blino, a Jesuit, was not equal to his task; he treated her ambitions very cavalierly.

"I want to be a saint, Father," she told him. "I want to love God as much as St. Teresa of Avila did."

"Be content to correct your faults and not to offend Him anymore."

"But it's not a rash wish," she persisted. "Didn't our Lord say, 'Be you therefore perfect as also your heavenly Father is perfect'?"

She took the Gospel literally. Come, come now! Father Blino could hardly believe his ears.

Another Jesuit, Father Pichon, arrived at the convent to give a retreat when the difficulties of her postulancy were at their highest, a moment when she was undergoing a crisis of doubt. For Thérèse used to doubt . . . Would these trifling contradictions and feeble human disappointments have hurt her so much if God had mingled with them some healing grace that she could feel? She had scarcely entered the convent when he was hidden from her eyes; the ordeal of abandonment by God came upon her at one blow, the very first day, and for no apparent reason; and it lasted for months on end, without intermission. "My spiritual daily bread was a bitter dryness." This was no exaggeration, for she wrote to Céline a month after going to the Carmel:

> It is hard entering on a day's work when Jesus hides away from one's love. What has become of that kind friend? Doesn't He see our misery and the burdens that we have to bear? Where is He? Why doesn't He come and encourage us?

But immediately she hastened to reassure her lonely sister:

> Don't be afraid, Céline; He is there, quite close, and watching us. He begs these trials and tears from us because He wants them for souls — for one's own soul; and He is preparing a great reward. I am sure He hates giving us this gall to drink, but He knows that it is the only way of preparing us *to know Him as He knows Himself and to become as gods ourselves* . . . We have to rise above everything that happens and keep this world at its distance: the air is cleaner higher up! Jesus may hide Himself, but He can always be found.

But if He persists in hiding? Thérèse courageously put a good face on things. Her sister should never be allowed to suffer as she had done.

The injustice and persecution of her fellow-creatures were of no importance, she told herself. She had come to this house of religion to seek her God, the Lord Jesus; and since she had already found Him outside, where she prayed so badly and loved so little, surely she would meet Him infinitely more closely and constantly under this chosen roof. But the Bridegroom did not come to the meeting-place He had appointed. Thérèse had entered Carmel for the sake of Jesus — and Jesus was not there. How could He be made to show His face?

A dry heart, dry eyes, prayers without savor and even without meaning, a diabolical aridity. Perhaps this was hell. No, it was only an anteroom of it. She did not yet deserve hell on earth, and it must be deserved to be inflicted. Thérèse began to wonder if she had not incurred the wrath of God; she questioned the worth of everything she did; she felt the tide of scrupulosity surging up again within her. At this juncture, Father Pichon came to the rescue.

Thérèse had met him the year before, in the parlor when she was visiting her sisters; she had mentioned her determination then, and he had encouraged it. He remembered her well and expected to find her a good little nun, "of childlike fervor," following a "smooth road." She confided in him only partially (she tells us that she found an "extreme difficulty in unburdening her soul"; this is a characteristic to be borne in mind, for it throws light on her life and destiny), but when the priest looked into the half-opened abyss, he was able to appreciate the dreadful depth of grace in suffering that was already hers. If she had not remained half-closed up, it is probable that he would have understood her completely. As it was, after a general confession in which Thérèse went over all her deficiencies, levities, and childish faults, he was constrained to declare with all solemnity "before God, our Lady, the angels, and the saints" that she had never been guilty of "a single deadly sin" — "but without any merit on your part," he added. For the rest, he declined to give an opinion. It is possible that the secret that she withheld from him, whether from shyness, modesty, or lack of words to express it, was beyond his competence or the little of it that his humility would allow to him. He told her that she was being tested. But he saw the work of the Holy Spirit in her and ended his instruction with the words: "My child, may our Lord always be your prior and novice-master!"

Thérèse rejoiced at the assurance that no sin had "soiled her baptismal garment" and without any merit on her part (she had attributed none to herself). She believed that peace had returned to her and that she had found a true spiritual father. But Father Pichon was sent to Canada.

Chapter Seven

The Holy Face

Thérèse could no longer find her Well-beloved either in prayer or in Communion, but she learned to discover Him in the superiors who disappointed her and were a stumbling-block — for they could disappoint and harass her only in His name. She had entered Carmel primarily so that she might be of service to the souls of others; it was therefore only fitting that she should not simply endure suffering, but seek it, welcome it, and love it. She had learned from her Lord that souls can be saved only by the cross, by crosses, great or small; and now the more she encountered, the more ready she was to take them up. This revolution in her soul, of which there had been premonitory signs from her childhood, was brought to pass by contemplation of the sacred face of Jesus.

The smiling features of the holy Child were suddenly superseded in her heart by a pale and blood-stained face, worn out of recognition and humiliated almost to nothingness. He was the most beautiful among the sons of men: the most darling in the manger, the best at the carpenter's bench; in youth and manhood one look from His eyes would enthrall hearts; the unutterable beauty of the Godhead shone through His naturally perfected humanity. That divinity was hidden, that humanity let itself be destroyed. He-Who-Is elected and required Himself to become as nothing in order to conquer us, to have us as His own, to reign unrivaled over us in the glory of a common redemption. Whoever wants to conquer, to possess, and to reign must first put himself to school. The greedy, proud, ambitious Thérèse, the little girl who took everything and nothing less, soon knew what was left for her to do — she must conceal and utterly empty herself. The key, the only key, to the possession of Being is not-to-be. And since that which is not has nothing to expect, hope for, or want, so Thérèse ceased to expect, hope, and want — or did so for the time being as little as possible, seeing that she had not yet attained the perfection of complete nothingness.

She set out to diminish herself, and it became her chief preoccupation; as her ambition and vehemence for conquest increased, she made herself less and less. The word *little* that she uses so much, both of her "way" and herself, is not an affectation or a literary trick; it expresses exactly the hardest and most heroic resolution that so forcefully spirited a being could ever conceive and carry through.

It is natural that, after the more or less trite moral tales and other devotional books (the *Imitation* excepted) that she had to be content with in her childhood, she should now look for spiritual nourishment in the most powerful works of mysticism. For two years, the writings of St. John of the Cross were her constant companions. She also read St. Teresa, but apparently less readily and consistently, consequently with less profit; the strong mental processes of her namesake were not suited to her intuitive nature. So there were seven mansions in the interior castle, were there? And four degrees of prayer? That did not matter much, provided she could attain them. The first Teresa knew how to love Jesus; the second asked only for the secret of that love. These hidden things were made clear to her by the shaded light, the enlightening obscurities, the impassioned and tender ardors of the poems and treatises of St. John of the Cross, which did not call for a systematized method — her understanding was not incapable of such, but it cramped her spirit. She threw herself into the fire, so to speak, and assimilated the element directly: to pray and pray, to love and love, to reduce herself to nothing and nothing and again nothing. She learned the same detachment from Father Surin's *Fondements de la Vie Spirituelle*. Later on, she would meditate solely on the sacred Scriptures, wherein can be found all truth, all wisdom, and all love. Thérèse had that simplicity of outlook that can seize the spirit that lies behind the letter directly, without groping or uncertainty: a single word was enough — *Jesus;* or an image — the Holy Face. For this reason, she was providentially kept from confidential advisers and spiritual directors. She struggled along the path of perfection more and more by herself, more and more simply, more and more stripped. "Who hath believed our report? . . . There is no beauty in him, nor comeliness."[8] Thérèse used often to say over that word of Isaiah; it sums up the mystery that she clung to, considering and testing it for the space of five years.

If God still remained hidden — and it was only by a *tour de force* that she found Him in the image of the Man of Sorrows — yet the world was always there to add to Thérèse's adversities. The links that bound her heart to human creatures had not slackened; she was not forgetful of her father or of her sisters who cherished their memories of the old days. After an unsuccessful postulancy with the Poor Clares, the diffident Léonie had come back home, much against her will. Céline had promised to join Thérèse and

[8] Isa. 53:1-2.

meanwhile, felt that she was living in an exile to which duty held her; the letters that Thérèse wrote to her during the early years in Carmel seem to me the most touching of her writings. I believe them to be the most direct and spontaneous documents about herself that she has given us; they seem a product of necessity, and are gentle, eager, and radiant without a trace of conscious literary composition. She who found it so difficult to talk about herself and who "had not much to say" to her elders in the convent turned to her old playmate, and in the parlor it was chiefly to Céline that she unbosomed herself and spoke of spiritual things.

So at Les Buissonnets, Céline wanted to be a saint, too, and M. Martin continued his upward path. He had almost recovered from his stroke, and after he had treated himself to a short holiday, he appeared one day at the convent in an unusual state of exaltation. His three daughters listened behind the curtained grille while he told them in general terms of the wonderful things that had happened to him in the church of our Lady where Thérèse was baptized at Alençon. He had been well repaid for his sacrifices, too well. His happiness was so great, he declared, that he had protested to God that it was too much; he could not go to Heaven like that; he must suffer something for God's sake. And he added, "I offered myself." It did not seem right to him that his pain should be thus transformed, so he called the Almighty to order. For whom he had offered himself up, his daughters never knew, but at his avowal Thérèse shuddered, remembering the veiled man by the wash-house. Shortly afterward, he had another stroke.

He got better, however, and was able to lead Thérèse to the altar in her bridal dress when she was clothed with the habit on January 10, 1889. Whether he should live long or die tomorrow, he was seeing her beloved face for the last time, on this most beautiful of occasions, when a young girl girdled with chastity gives herself to that Bridegroom for whom she will remain forever maiden. Whiteness had a strong appeal for the candid Thérèse, and she wished that everything could be as white as her veil and gown, hoping that her friend the winter (she was born in January) would do her the favor of covering the earth with a garment of the snow that she loved so much. But the weather was mild. With his "little queen" on his arm, M. Martin wept and beamed. "It was his great day," says Thérèse. He knew that Céline, too, would become a Carmelite and that Léonie would not stay outside a convent, so he had given all his children to God; and God honored him by choosing these brides from his house. It remained only to give himself — and he was already given.

As Thérèse was lost to sight in the enclosure, the bishop inadvertently intoned the *Te Deum;* a priest reminded him that this is sung only at professions, but he saw fit to continue the hymn of praise. Meanwhile, through the window behind the statue of the child Jesus which, as usual and more than usual, she had decked with flowers, Thérèse saw that the cloister-garth was covered in snow.

She compares this day of exaltation with Palm Sunday; for her father as for her heavenly Bridegroom, the moment of triumph had to be swiftly followed by a passion. While she was putting on the brown tunic and novice's white veil, she saw ahead the hard road that the veiled man must tread. Almost exactly a month later, M. Martin had a third stroke and had at once to be taken to hospital, where general paralysis destroyed his will, his memory, and his understanding, leaving perhaps sufficient consciousness to make him aware of his state.

The blow had fallen. Thérèse repeated the homesick line of St. John of the Cross: "The dewy unspoiled dawns are gone." There was no longer anything but suffering to be looked forward to in this world. And it was not enough to be resigned to it.

Resignation is an enforced acquiescence; it has no depth of generosity, and to be of any use, it needs to be reinforced by an attempt to forget or at the very least by a tendency toward a passive state not far removed from indifference. The popular wisdom which men call "being philosophical," and which is well summed up in the short formula "Don't bother," is unworthy of a strong-souled person. It is not a matter of forgetting the ordeal which some loved one has to bear, and which we have to bear with him, but rather, the contrary: its reality has got to be deepened. We have to hold to it with all our affective powers, will it in the degree that God wills it, love it as God loves us when He permits the trial to come upon us. Then and only then will it become a joy, a crucifying happiness, in the same measure that it is our cross. All the saints have displayed the paradox of coexisting sorrow and joy, following the pattern of Christ, who knew in His agony the extremest anguish of a man and the highest exaltation of God.

Thérèse never ceased to think of her father, of her sisters lingering in the world, and of those secluded in the cloister; but at the same time, she made her own the seemingly cruel will of her Bridegroom and was able to write, "Ours is indeed an enviable lot and the seraphim in Heaven are jealous of our happiness! . . . God must love our father very much. He has begun his martyrdom. We too must go into the arena and offer up our sorrows . . . Let us suffer in peace." On this last word, she says, "To speak of peace is not the same as to speak of joy, or at least, of *joy that is felt*."

But what is an unfelt joy? Whatever it is, Thérèse flourished on it and was satisfied with it; it was like wine to her. She had a frightening artificial willed happiness, which was sustained by a grace that had neither sweetness nor savor. When she was deep in the waters of tribulation, without consolation in Heaven or earth, she could call herself, with a sincerity that equaled her audacity, "the happiest of people." Later, she even dared to write of these sad days, "The three years of my father's martyrdom seem to me the most pleasant and fruitful of our life. I would not exchange them for the most sublime ecstasies."

This reversal of values was gradually being brought about. Thérèse was becoming strong because she renounced the use of her strength, because she felt herself weak and wanted to be weak, a *little* flower blown by the wind, a *little* grain of sand borne on by the tide. She measured herself now only by God and so, day by day, became more conscious of her weakness and littleness. It is even a happiness, she says, "to carry one's crosses weakly." If we carry them at all, it is only because God helps us, and the less we count on our own strength, the more He will give us of His." "My God, my God, why hast thou forsaken me?" was the cry of Jesus from the Cross — precisely in order that the man in Him might give place to God, who brings everything out of nothing, who raises the dead and makes them live again. Thérèse would not take her eyes from those of the Man of Sorrows, the despised and most abject of men.

As the prophetic veil that had hidden the face of her mysterious visitor was a figure of the cloud that was now over her father's mind, so Thérèse approximated it to the blood-stained mask of tears and sweat that covers the Sacred Face of Christ; M. Martin had been chosen to receive the marks of Christ's humiliation and be thereby its living image for his daughters.[9] The time had now come for her to add a new title of nobility to that which she

[9] See Father Henry Petitot, O.P., *St. Teresa of Lisieux: A Spiritual Renaissance*, trans. the Benedictine Dames of Stanbrook (London, 1927).

proudly bore already. She must henceforward be not only Thérèse of the Child Jesus but also "of the Holy Face." The mother prioress, who was watching her develop and increase and who, while continuing to nag at her, valued and loved her ("She is the best of my good sisters, an angel," she declared in private), offered no objection to this wish. This double name of Thérèse should not be forgotten, as it often is; it synthesizes the economy of our salvation from Bethlehem and Nazareth to Calvary, and unites in her the perfection of innocence with the sublimity of grief. Moreover, it is from the cross that the "way of childlikeness" takes its beginning.

The time drew on for her profession, which normally takes place a year after clothing. She still received afflictions from the world and dryness from God, living between an abyss and a desert. She persevered in obedience, in humility, in the daily usage of sisterly charity, and the more she suffered, the more she corresponded with suffering. As this began to be noticed, people turned to her in their needs, and when a novice was in difficulties, the prioress would send her to Thérèse for comfort and encouragement. That she was ahead of her companions was doubted by nobody except the superior, Canon Delatroette. He suffered from the great weakness of insisting that he was always right, and accordingly formally opposed her profession on the due date, demanding that it should be put off for another eight months. This act of injustice was almost too much for Thérèse. She had looked forward longingly to her profession, and rightly so, for it would be a token that her offering was accepted and that she was bound forever. Now she was overwhelmed by despair, at grips with her instinct to rebel . . .

However, while she was meditating after a reading of Father Surin, she was enlightened by the Spirit of God and saw her error. Her urgent wish to take her vows "appeared to her to be mixed with much self-esteem." She discerned in it less desire to please our Lord than satisfaction at going up a step and receiving official and public acknowledgment of her deserts, and also some fear lest people should say, "There you are! The little sister who aims at being a saint is not able even to keep up with the others," for it is very likely that, in spite of her goodness and the severity that was shown toward her, perhaps because of them, she had raised a certain amount of jealousy; there were some who took advantage of her gentleness and thought by being hard toward her to please the prioress.

So Thérèse resigned herself: she would go on being humiliated, laughed at, and chaffed; she was used to it. It was God's will. He was delaying her profession because she was not yet worthy of it. "I will wait as long as You wish," she told Him, "only I cannot bear to think that my union with You should be put off through my fault. I will try my hardest to make myself a glorious garment of diamonds and precious stones, and when You see it is good enough, I know that nothing will stop You from taking me for Your bride."

She went to work at once and scrutinized her every action relentlessly, congratulating herself on being still so imperfect and having so much yet to do for amendment and purification. She reflected on the three vows of religion and saw that she conformed to them very inadequately, especially in the matter of poverty. Truly she had nothing in her possession except necessaries authorized by the rule, but she regarded them with an affection like that given to old friends. Her bare cell was dear to her, and she liked to see it very clean and tidy — with nothing missing. She thought her plain little jug very pretty, in shape, color, and material; when she came back from Compline, she would put her lamp on the table — she was fond of that lamp, too — and sometimes read the *Living Flame of Love* or the prophets or the Gospels, and that was an hour of real peace. Now she began to wonder if to take delight in what she had and saw and read was properly compatible with the poverty she had undertaken.

That pretty jug was taken away; so much the better. It was replaced by a heavy cracked one; better still. She extended her love to the "ugliest and most inconvenient things." One evening, she could not find her lamp, and she had to go without her reading, so she sat in the dark and experienced the joy of having absolutely nothing. She found plenty of such little ways of deepening her spirit of poverty; when she did anything for anybody, she hated it to be noticed; she willingly accepted blame that was properly due to others; she folded and put away cloaks that were lying about; when the fault for a broken vase was wrongly put on her, she kissed the ground and promised to be more careful. She deliberately attached herself to a very difficult lay-sister novice, who rudely rejected her kindness, but Thérèse persevered with tireless patience and in the end, the cross-grained sister became a devoted and gentle friend.

In the same spirit, she offered to look after old Sister Saint Peter, another lay-sister, who had been soured by ill-health and had to be led to and from the refectory. Nobody volunteered for this job, and Thérèse herself hesitated, but the more she disliked the idea of it, the more imperious the duty appeared. And it was a business! First of all Sister Saint Peter's seat had to be arranged in a certain way to enable her to get up, which she could not do without help. Then she had to be followed gingerly, supported by a hand on her girdle, and at the least false step, she growled, "You're going too fast! You'll have me over and break my neck!" If, on the other hand, there was an excess of circumspection, she would think there was no support, and complain, "I can't feel your hand; you're letting me go! I said you were too young to look after me!"

There was more business in the refectory, to get her set down at table and her sleeves arranged, again in a special way. One day Thérèse noticed that she had difficulty in cutting her bread, so for the future, she cut it for her and never left her without a sweet smile.

With such jewels as these did Thérèse adorn her bridal-gown, and the Bridegroom who gave them alone saw them. Nevertheless, her retreat preparatory for profession was an occasion of cruel aridity, which she strove to be content with and to explain. It was her custom to clothe her dereliction in figures and symbols after the manner of the *Song of Songs* and the poems of St. John of the Cross. She had a keen imagination and doubtless the Holy Spirit energized in it, but it must be carefully noted that the purposes she attributes to God and the communication that she receives from Him are drawn simply from her own faith and not from any explicit revelation; they have nothing in common with the *real* conversations between St. Catherine of Siena and her Lord. The following is a letter she wrote to her sister Pauline (Agnes of Jesus) in September 1890:

> My dearest mother,
>
> Your little solitary must tell you all about her travels.
>
> Before I set out, my Well-beloved asked me to what country I should like to go and by which route, and I answered that I had only one wish and that was to reach the top of the Mountain of Love.
>
> Then I saw several roads before me but I did not feel I could choose any one of them wholeheartedly, for each had so many advantages . . .
>
> So our Lord led me by the hand into an underground passage which is neither hot nor cold and where there is no

> sun or rain or wind; I cannot see anything except a half-hidden glow, and that glow comes from the eyes of Jesus looking down on me.
>
> He says nothing to me or I to Him, except that I love Him more than myself, and I feel within me that it is so with Him, for I am more His than my own.
>
> I can't see whether we are getting toward the end of our journey because we are traveling underground, but somehow it seems to me that we are coming to the top of the mountain.
>
> I am thankful to Jesus for making me walk in this darkness, where I have a very deep peace, and I will gladly pass the rest of my days in this dim underworld — I ask only that my darkness shall bring light to sinners.
>
> I am glad, yes, very glad, to have no consolations. I should be ashamed were my love to be like that of those girls in the world who are always looking at the hands of their fiancées to see if they have brought any presents, or study their faces to catch a loving smile that will give them pleasant feelings . . .
>
> At all costs, I must pluck the martyr's palm of St. Agnes, if not by blood, then by love.

She says elsewhere, "I do not want love that I can feel; if Jesus can feel it, then that is enough."

On the eve of her profession, just as hope was reviving, a furious storm, the most furious of her life, broke over Thérèse's soul: Her "call" was a pretense, she was deceiving herself, deceiving her fellows, her superiors, God Himself; her vocation was a snare, a dream, idle fancy, a lie told from pride, and it would be sacrilegious to go on. She must leave the convent at once.

She sprang up, surprised the novice-mistress by calling her from the chapel, and poured out her distress to her. Mother Mary of the Angels met this crowning humiliation with laughter, and thereby freed Thérèse from the trap that was laid for her. "From the morning of September 8, I was borne away on a flood of peace, and in that peace beyond words I took the holy vows."

On that occasion, she asked God to grant, according to His will, all that she had a right to wish for on earth: in the first place, the acceptance of her full offering of herself; then, the welfare of her convent, the good estate of Céline, the entrance of Léonie into the order of the Visitation; finally, at the most solemn moment, that her father should be cured — "because mother prioress told me to ask this," she added humbly. Didn't she want her father to recover? Unquestionably she did. But since he had offered himself, she was doubtful if she ought to try to deprive God of his sacrifice.

The lovely weather was suitable to the day. An eyewitness declares that during the procession, a great flight of swallows passed over the convent, skimming the walls so closely that some of the nuns with an eye for omens took it to be a sign from Heaven. And Thérèse's demands were imperial: she called on her King instantaneously to convert all sinners to Him and to call from Purgatory every soul that was detained therein!

A fortnight later, she received the black veil, but M. Martin was not present. Night again enveloped her.

The eldest of her cousins, Joan Guérin, got married, and the attention that she lavished on her husband filled Thérèse with jealousy and shame. If a woman could do all that for a mortal man, what ought she not to do for her heavenly Bridegroom? To bind herself more closely to Him, she amused herself with drawing up, on the model of her cousin's wedding card, an ingenuous invitation to the "spiritual marriage of Jesus with Sister Thérèse on Mount Carmel." She had to divert her mind — with mere childishness, if you will. She *must* appear happy and cheerful; for the bride of the Most High to go about with a mournful face would be tantamount to a declaration that He was unkind to her — hence, the too-flowery garlands that adorn the most distressing avowals in *The Story of a Soul*.

It is to be noted that while God withheld everything during the daytime He gave her entrancing dreams at night: again, she saw those works of nature that she loved so much, flowers, brooks, and trees, the sea and "pretty little children"; she caught butterflies and birds, of unknown species but worthy of the Earthly Paradise. The stroke of five o'clock broke the spell, and in the cold and gloomy choir, her savorless prayers began again.

The general retreat in 1891 brought peace for a while. Formal retreats did not appeal to Thérèse: the preachers' words did not make much impression, and her mind had difficulty in following their meaning. She had to be all the time struggling with a sense of constraint, of boredom, probably of embarrassment, and she tended to disregard the formal reasons for loving God; for they seemed a limitation of love or even a positive hindrance. But she does not speak of these things very clearly; mortification was making her more and more reticent. However, if a preacher is to be judged by the spiritual enlargement and deepening that he produces among his hearers, Father Alexis, a Franciscan from the friary at Caen, must be accounted to have spoken with the voice of the Holy Spirit, for on this occasion, Thérèse was touched from the very first word; she felt that she was understood even before she had spoken to him.

For the first time in her life, she was able to open her soul to a superior, and the counsels of Father Alexis satisfied and freed her. "He launched me full-sail upon the ocean of trust and love which had called to me so strongly without my daring to venture upon it." What eased her mind more than anything else was to learn that "my faults were not a cause of any sorrow to God." She had vaguely felt that this was so, that God's mercy regards our nothingness and is ceaselessly tempering divine justice, but hitherto nobody had said this to her, or at least not with sufficient authority to command belief. She knew well enough that God would forgive anything in others — but not in her, because of that special love of which she was the chosen object and of which she had received tokens. It was a revelation to her that she need fear God no more. All her troubles had arisen from a certain constraint, but now she was free to love without bounds and without fear. "My temperament is such," she writes, "that fear makes me waver and draw back; but with love I don't merely go forward: I fly."

Chapter Eight

The Little Way

Thérèse was eighteen when she exchanged the white veil of promise for the black veil, crucifix, and large rosary of the wedded brides, but she asked for and was given permission to remain with the novices. She wore a worn-out tunic of rough serge, and her feet were protected from the cold only by sandals fastened with hemp. As she never complained, the oldest cast-off and patched garments were allotted to her, and when a dish of food was burnt or spoiled, it was a standing joke that "that was good enough for Sister Thérèse." She did not seem to notice, and nobody ever knew what she liked and what she didn't.

She added almost nothing to the austerities imposed by the rule, but these she observed to the letter — for example, taking the discipline three times a week. She was not afraid to administer this severely; the pain of it for her did not reside in that. At the beginning of her novitiate, she was anxious to multiply such mortifications, on which the prioress, being physically strong, was keen. But Thérèse discovered that the Devil makes his bit out of them, because after giving oneself sharp correction, one reckons to have made full amends, and moreover, it is flattering to see oneself as a sort of

Father of the Desert. It seemed to her that those nuns who used nettles for their voluntary penances were not always the best religious.

So she was content to wear a cross covered with prickles next her skin; but she was not sure that even that was not a source of some vanity, and when it caused a sore to form, she gave it up. All that, she thought, had better be left to great saints, who never gloried in it, as such trifles could not satisfy them. Theirs was the "great way," and her pride made her suspicious of it. It was precisely because she was made of the stuff of such as St. Agnes and St. Sebastian and Joan of Arc and Catherine of Siena that she tried to be like them only in their smallest, humblest, most hidden ways. She would readily rescue the Pope, save her country, give her life in martyrdom — but she was not asked to. Striking deeds are out of place in a convent, where one's only business is to be pleasing to God and so to save souls, many souls, and if need be, to set before them a practical and practicable example fitted to the requirements of the times. After all, she was only an obscure lower-middle-class girl, whose life in "the world" had promised no more than a commonplace career consisting of the careful performance of domestic duties, and in that respect, there was little enough difference in her present state.

Accordingly, she found a way of holiness equally commonplace, in the exact observance of the rule, and followed it steadily, weaving her life, thread by thread, out of insignificant actions that were too small for notice or record. But God saw them and, as each was weighted with love, valued them equally with the martyrdom of St. Cecilia, the foundations of St. Teresa, or the triumphs of St. Francis. The very fact that they were too small to be an object of self-satisfaction increased their worth.

That was Sister Thérèse's "little way." Actually she had been pursuing it for a long time, ever since that far-off day when her aunt had given her a string of beads wherewith to keep count of her "good deeds." She no longer counted them, for they now followed one another as swiftly as the seconds of time: she was reaping the harvest of her childhood's self-discipline.

While she was a postulant, she had been put to look after the linen, and had as well a staircase and dormitory to keep clean and the vegetables to gather and bring in daily. After she was clothed, she was assigned to the refectory under the direct supervision of her sister Pauline, with whom she would not allow herself to speak except when necessity required. As she had had little training in housework and was not so strong as she looked, she found the work a strain, but would not let anybody see it.

In addition, she undertook any unpleasant jobs that the others were glad to avoid: laundering clothes by a hot stove in summer, washing up in cold water in midwinter, which gave her chilblains and chapped hands (she suffered a great deal from the cold, but nobody knew it until after she was dead). It is said that when a nun clumsily splashed her with dirty water, Sister Thérèse did not bat an eyelid. She had learned to control any movement that would draw attention to herself; she would not wipe the sweat from her face, rub her hands together, drag her feet or show any other sign of fatigue, so that no one should see that she was hot or cold or tired or ill; she could completely control her tears, and smile or laugh when she felt inclined to cry. She seemed to be the cheerfulest nun in the house, and therefore passed for the happiest. Once, when pinning on her scapular, a sister stuck a pin deep into Thérèse's shoulder without noticing what she had done; Thérèse hardly moved and, so as not to make her companion sorry, went about her work as if nothing had happened.

God everywhere and in everything; a constant endeavor to be pleasing in His eyes, and to require nothing of Him except the means so to be; the least turning toward Him is its own reward. It seems sometimes as if He is not there. But He is there whenever we think of Him, in the thinking brain, in the loving heart, in the determination to do His will. In a life whose every sentiment and every action is directed to His service, and consequently filled with Him, there is no delight or consolation left to be desired. It is exactly the contrary of *non serviam*.

The soul is led by love as a child by the hand of his father. The child can shut his eyes; it does not matter whether he sees his father or not. Thérèse's soul could not see Jesus, but her love found Him at every step. But that she loved did not prove to her that she was loved, and when she doubted it, she was overcome by a frightful dejection. On one of these black days, only two months after Father Alexis's retreat, she put on a smiling face and went to the infirmary to visit that Mother Genevieve who did not understand her but whom she held in veneration. Mother Genevieve was dying.

"Listen, my child," she said to Thérèse, "I've only one thing to say to you . . . Serve God in peace and joy; remember always that He is the God of peace." Her cautions and warnings notwithstanding, Mother Genevieve had seen into her soul and spoken the word that was needed.

Thérèse was present when she died. It was the first death she had witnessed, and she found it "a beautiful sight." She felt "filled with an unspeakable happiness and elation," as though Heaven had opened and shown her a beam of its light. She soaked up the dying woman's last tear in a piece of cambric. A few days later, she dreamed that Mother Genevieve was distributing presents among the nuns; to Thérèse she gave nothing, but said to her three times over, "To you I leave my heart." In death, holiness had recognized a saint. With such tokens of love had Thérèse to be satisfied.

M. Martin's health did not improve, and he was moved from Les Buissonnets to a house in the town nearby M. Guérin's. Céline was increasingly alone and clung more and more to Thérèse, who took the opportunity to teach her the love that she herself practiced, which never wearied, even though God ever disappointed her.

In the same year, 1891, Thérèse had the very great happiness of being removed from the service of the refectory to that of the sacristy. She handled the linen, the vestments, the sacrificial vessels, the wafers that were to become the body of the Well-beloved, with trembling fingers. Before putting the altar-breads into the ciborium, she would look at herself reflected in its shining interior, not to see her face but to leave its image there where it would touch Him who was to be therein. One day after Mass, she noticed a tiny fragment of the consecrated bread left on the paten. It was to her a measure of the humility and loving-kindness of the Bridegroom who, wholly and entirely there, had let Himself be forgotten expressly for her, in a form infinitely small, the smallest that would yet enable them to meet. She knelt and worshiped; she called her fellows to worship with her.

While Thérèse was quietly and unobtrusively fulfilling her responsible duties, toward the end of December, an epidemic of *grippe*, which was raging under the new name of "influenza," reached Lisieux and attacked the convent. It spared only two of the nuns (Thérèse had it very lightly), and the less sick had to nurse the others: the whole house became a hospital. Sister Thérèse was in sole charge of the chapel, and the rest of her time, she nursed the unfortunate victims. She had to face everything. There were three deaths, one after the other, and she ministered in their last moments, first to the sub-prioress, Mother Mary of the Angels, and then to Sister Madeleine, who had no one else to tend her. These sisters answering the call and going to God with a smiling face taught Thérèse to love death. She wanted to die like that.

Throughout the epidemic, she was allowed to receive Holy Communion every day, a privilege rare at that time when daily Communion had not yet become customary. It might be supposed that in an atmosphere of danger and of active charity and prayer, with those serene and glad deaths before her eyes, her love would have expanded and blossomed, but she found herself incapable of really fervent thanksgiving for the daily coming of her Lord. She expressed it in her actions but not in her heart, so she called on the angels to supply in her for what she was doing so inadequately. During this time, the awesome Canon Delatroette was able to see Sister Thérèse in action and his prejudices vanished, but she was now beyond appreciating any approbation which did not come directly from Heaven.

When this trial was over and normal community life began again, Thérèse returned to her "little way," helping her sisters, encouraging Céline, neither more nor less happy than before. This is how she speaks of her latest discovery, fruit of the community retreat of 1892, taking as text the words of our Lord to Zaccheus: "Make haste and come down, for this day I must abide in thy house."[10]

> Jesus tells us to come down. Where, then, are we to go . . . Our Lord wants us to take Him into our hearts, which are doubtless empty of created things. But alas! *mine is not empty of myself*, and that is why He tells me to come down. And I want to come down, low, very low, so that Jesus can rest His divine head on my heart and know that He is understood and loved.

[10]Luke 19:5.

Thérèse humbled herself to get away from self — and met self at every turn. She gave her "we" a hard time of it. But she had to come down still further, until she reached an infinity of lowliness.

In June 1892, another sacristan was appointed, and Thérèse was for the time being out of work. The prioress suggested that she should try her hand at painting, and it is likely that Sister Agnes coached her, for Pauline had a schoolgirl's gift for painting, especially miniatures, of a kind suitable to a "magazine for young ladies."

I have said what must be thought about these unpretentious efforts, which were just to the taste of the *bourgeoisie* at its worst and consequently equally acceptable to both sisters. We must look at their intention.

As I have shown, Thérèse had exceptional sensibility, which, had she been better informed and directed, might have blossomed fruitfully, if not in painting then in poetry. She knew how to think in images, her senses were keen, and she had something to say. So, in accordance with orders, she took pencil and brush and astonished everybody by producing quite good colored pictures, "nice," carefully finished off, in which flowers rained and cherubs fluttered. She had never studied the works of "the masters" in picture-galleries or had any training of mind and eye and she remained faithful to the ideas of her schoolmistresses, innocently imitating the things she had seen and had had recommended to her as worthy of admiration — collections of pious pictures, magazine illustrations, First-Communion cards.

They were such a success that she was entrusted with the decoration of an oratory and was assigned to work in the studio, where she remained four years, at the same time being in charge of the hatch. Her modest pictures were works of art only in the eyes of the nuns; for us they are relics, things into which she put much love.[11]

A year later, she was revealed as a poetess. Nobody can deny that she could write. When her prose is stripped of its pious rhetoric and deliberate childishness, the wreaths and cascades of flowers, it is found to be strong, clear, straightforward, and to the point, showing the influence of the Bible and sometimes lit up by lightning-flashes like those of St. John of the Cross — when they are not taken directly from him. This easy and harmonious style is the vehicle of high thought, as a rereading of the end of *The Story of a Soul* and especially of her letters shows. I shall come back to this, for at the moment I am considering her verse. Sister Agnes rhymed as well as painted, hymns, occasional pieces, and so on, and as no one could miss Sister Thérèse's poetical fancy — you had only to hear her telling stories — the prioress told her again to emulate Pauline. She did not have to be told a second time.

The first of her extant efforts, dated February 2, 1893, is called "Divine Dew, or Mary's Maiden Milk," and was written to be sung to the well-known tune *Noël d'Adam*. They are nearly all like that. The musical repertory of the Carmelites at recreation on feast-days extended from carols to laments and from laments to romantic "ballads," from *Plainte du Mousse* to *Petit soulier de Noël*, even, in their boldness, from the most *risqué* songs of Niedermeyer to Holmès, from Ambrose Thomas to Massenet, from the air *Connais-tu le pays? to Sérénade du Passant*, songs that were then current at provincial parties and even in Paris. It was these tunes of very doubtful merit that had to sustain Thérèse's religious inspiration

[11]They can be judged from the one called the "Dream of the Child Jesus," which is kept at the Visitation convent of Le Mares and reproduced in the French edition of *The Story of a Soul*.

and carry the praises of God to Heaven. It is understandable, up to a point, that the asceticism in music imposed by their rule for the choir-office — all the psalms are monotoned — led to a reaction at the times when the nuns were free from this discipline: there was a debauch of sentimentality and worldly frippery, and the young ladies of the community sang the songs that they knew in the way they had learned when they were "in society"; however, God looks at the heart.

But poetry was bound to suffer in such circumstances, and it would be highly unjust to judge Thérèse's verse simply as poetry; it is verse that was meant to be sung, and sung to unsuitable, not to say inappropriate, airs that were mostly commonplace and devastatingly sentimental.

In my opinion, it is a marvel that she was able occasionally to safeguard the real gift of poetry that she had implicitly fostered since her childhood. She displays excessive slickness, maddening wordiness, and a complete lack of discrimination in her use of words, phrases, times, and images; on the other hand, there is her will to say out the things that were in her heart and to express the vigorous and exact thoughts that she had drawn from Christian doctrine, the Bible, and the writings of the mystics, deepened and enriched by her inner use of them. There is always disproportion between her songs and their poetic substance, but suddenly the purring stops and the thing becomes untrammeled and clear, nothing but the thought is left: she has momentarily found its form, its literary equivalent. She does not reach the incomparable starkness of Racine's *Cantiques spirituels*, but you are reminded of them and are sorry that Thérèse had no competent and careful guidance when she wrote, for she might have excelled some of the acknowledged poets in the France of her day.

Au nom de Celui que j'adore,
Mes soeurs, je viens tendre la main
Et chanter pour l'Enfant divin
Car il ne peut parler encore . . .

Il ne peut parler . . . He did not speak to her: Thérèse sang for Him; and to her dying day, she sang His songs, however poor and inadequate those songs might be. At times of aridity, when she had no strength left to pray, the faith that was slipping from her and the love that she did not feel were rekindled by the necessity of making a carol or a cantata for some "occasion" — Christmas recreation, the prioress's nameday, the lay-sisters' festival, or the profession of a novice. When her spirit was emptied, her songs filled it; when it was too full, they enabled it to overflow. They were a grace that God gave when all others were withheld, and it is easy to see how she came to write so much verse in four years. It was produced with little effort, and she made no boast of it; she was "allowed to do good to a few souls" by it. That was the explanation and, indeed, the only object of her writing. Later on, she told the novices, "to answer directly you are called is worth more than thinking about beautiful and holy things or writing books about the lives of saints" — to say nothing of writing poetry!

Sister Thérèse took up no superior attitude about external works; she had dreamed of being a missionary, converting the heathen by word and deed, and Céline tells us that she hesitated before choosing a contemplative order. But from now on, she put a far higher value on the efficacy of interior works, self-denial, and prayer. "The most difficult task of all is the one that has to be undertaken within oneself, self-conquest . . . That *living death* is worth more for the salvation of souls than all the others put together."

She spoke truly. The disdain in which some Catholics hold the contemplative orders shows a complete incomprehension of the hidden economy of the universe. Prayer is its center, and prayer involves love and selflessness. The posthumous apostolate of Sister Thérèse of Lisieux is a striking proof. Meanwhile, she went on, still going down in order that we might go up.

The priorate of Mother Mary of Gonzaga came to an end in February 1893, and Mother Agnes of Jesus was elected in her place. She saw fit to appoint the former prioress novice-mistress, both as a graceful compliment and to give scope to her energy (which, as we have seen, was devouring). But Mother Agnes had her doubts about Mother Mary's rough and capricious ways in an office that requires a delicate touch, and so named Thérèse as her assistant. That shows what Pauline thought of her sister, but it also put Thérèse in a most unenviable position, between the Devil (so to say), Mother Mary, and the deep sea, the novices. Would the new mistress, full of years and experience, put up with a twenty-year-old sister taking a part in the training of her novices? It is true that Thérèse's perseverance had softened Mother Mary, who admired and was fond of her, while Thérèse, so far from having any grudge, was grateful for her needful severity and added a real affection to the respect in which she held Mother Mary. Nevertheless, these amiable dispositions were no guarantee against collisions, and there was ample opportunity for Thérèse to demonstrate that submission to God's will brings daily help in difficulties. It is not known how she was able to adjust her views to those of her superior without damage resulting to the souls they had to care for together.

That she had much to suffer is certain. We are assured that she alone was effectively the novice-mistress, and we must believe it. But it seems all but impossible that Mother Mary of Gonzaga should have abdicated into her hands. She must have guided from afar and, from time to time, swooped down suddenly on her charges, producing a confusion that only the Holy Spirit could repair.

Sister Thérèse now had five daughters, five souls for which she was responsible, and on the day of her promotion, she was overcome by a sense of her insufficiency. She put herself in the hands of God, "You see, Lord, that I am too small to bring up Your children. If it is Your will that I should give them what they need, fill my hands, and I will give Your gifts to all who come to me for nourishment, without leaving Your arms or even turning my head." "When I understood," she adds, "that I could do nothing by myself, my task seemed more simple. Interiorly I occupied myself with becoming more and more united to God, knowing all the rest would be added to that." She returns again and again to union with God by lessening of self, and she taught it and made it real to her novices.

I have emphasized that during these long years of convent life, Sister Thérèse not only experienced no ecstasies, raptures, supernatural communications, or interior consolations, but most of the time even had no sense of God's presence. Nevertheless, she remained united to Him. It can hardly be supposed that her human will to believe, to hope, and to love was alone sufficient to keep her in health of mind and heart on this implacably austere road; God's grace upheld her faith, hope, and love from moment to moment. Her loving contemplation of Him may not have brought her any sensible joy, but it filled her with vigor, and the more she mortified herself, the more life-giving was the grace she received; all the gifts of the Holy Spirit were freely hers, especially wisdom and fortitude. She made full use of them, without hesitancy or premeditation. She had learned to be strong and wise without desperate labor, but that was not enough if she was to weather the storm. There is a certain point of forsakenness when human wisdom and strength must fail, even though they are solidly based and reinforced by the remembered experience of an absolute reality. Thérèse's past life told her that God was her friend; she knew from the Christian faith that He was always with her; but this double reserve of assurance would have been used up long since if the inexhaustible stores of grace had not been at her disposal. Or rather, her spiritual treasury was empty — Thérèse was no miser — and God fed her from day to day "with a new kind of food."

"I found it within me," she writes, "without knowing how it got there. I simply believe that it was Jesus Himself, hidden at the bottom of my poor little heart, acting on me in some mysterious way and inspiring me to do whatever He wished to be done at any given moment" — whatever He wished her to do and feel and think and endure and love.

In this way, she was able to carry on herself and to direct the paths of others, her novices. To the best of her knowledge and ability, her acts were God's acts, God's thoughts were her thoughts. It can scarcely be said that God was withholding Himself.

Chapter Nine

The Story of a Soul

The last time that M. Martin was able to be taken to the parlor of the convent, he was clearly near his end, muttering incoherently and almost unrecognizable. When the time came to take leave of his daughters, he raised his eyes and his hand, one finger outstretched, choking with sobs. So he remained for a long time, able to say only the words, "In Heaven! In Heaven!"

Surely he went straight there. Sister Thérèse had not a doubt of it when he died on July 29, 1894, near Evreux, at a house where M. Guérin spent his holidays. Léonie had gone to the Visitation convent at Le Mans, so only Céline was with him. Hope was mixed with her grief: this death broke her last earthly tie, and she was free to join Mary, Pauline, and Thérèse in Carmel. Thérèse took the death of "her king" very bravely; she was glad for his release and prayed to him as one prays to a saint. She asked him that God would allow her a sign in testimony of her father's heavenly bliss, of which she felt so certain, and that that sign should be Céline's entry into Carmel.

Some of the nuns were not altogether pleased by the prospect of a fourth recruit to reinforce the "Martin party." We have seen how careful Thérèse was not to take advantage of having relatives in the convent, and her sisters recognized that this apparent "standoffishness" arose from her desire for perfection and careful conformity with the Carmelite rule. There was, therefore, no ground for fear that the presence of Céline would encourage the formation of a family caste that might be tempted to control the community. The opposition was led by a venerable nun (her name is not recorded) whose opinion carried weight, and she seemed adamant. It would have been awkward for the prioress, Agnes of Jesus, to plead the cause of her own sister too warmly, so Céline's chances were looking bad, and Sister Thérèse turned to God with a fervid appeal that was almost a demand. As she was returning from her thanksgiving after Communion, she met the hostile nun, who told her with tears that she had reconsidered the matter and that she was strongly in favor of Céline's request being granted. This did away with any hesitation on the part of the bishop, and he had only to give his permission. M. Martin had answered; he was living among the blessed.

"What a happiness it is to find him as he was in the old days and more fatherly than ever!" wrote Thérèse to Céline on August 19. "He has been in Heaven only a month, and all your wishes are fulfilled." This was probably the last time that Thérèse "used a pen to speak with her dear sister." "Come," she says to her. "We will suffer together," and adds, "*Then Jesus will take one of us*, and the others will stop in exile for a short time."

Was this an obscure foreboding or the effect of an explicit revelation? The disease that eventually carried her off does not seem yet to have made itself felt, but she returns to the subject: "Don't worry about my prophecy, it's only a joke. I'm not ill; I've got an iron constitution — *but the Lord can break iron as easily as earthenware*."

Thérèse compared herself to a "little hound," who "runs after the hare" from morning until night. The prioress and the senior novice-mistress were the huntsmen: they could not "run in the undergrowth," but a young hound like her could get in anywhere, "and she had a good nose." She kept a close eye on her little hares; she wished them no harm, but while she licked them, she "told them all the truth about themselves," trying "to make of them what the huntsman wanted." On September 14, she had one more leveret, called Céline "in the world" and, in religion, Sister Genevieve of the Holy Face.

Some time before, Céline had accepted an invitation to a ball on the occasion of a wedding; rather against her inclination, certainly, but a girl's inclinations are apt to be deceiving, and one dance is sometimes enough to make her forget that she is already promised elsewhere. A young man asked her for the first dance, and they took the floor together. But Thérèse was praying. Then an unbelievable thing happened: neither of them could move; their feet seemed to be riveted to the floor. It was an absurd situation, and with one accord, they gave up the idea of dancing and took a stroll instead. Henceforward Céline was not tempted by the pleasures of the world, and her sister urged her to have no wish at all except to "love Jesus to distraction." The love of God is unquestionably exacting, but, as St. John of the Cross says, it "acts so powerfully that it can draw good from anything" — even from a ball.

In the direction of novices Sister Thérèse showed a natural and supernatural common sense and balance, firmness, and understanding that surprised the sisters. She was gentle with her charges, managing them skillfully and sinking her own personal ideas in order not to hamper anyone in developing along the lines that suited her. This cost her something, for she knew by experience that her "little way" was much the best; but when necessary, she recommended another, trusting to God to bring the novice around to it by this other road. What hurt her most was to have to watch and correct shortcomings in others when she herself was so imperfect. But it had to be done, and she let nothing pass; as soon as a fault was noticed, she waged war to the death against it.

A religious must not form particular friendships, even with her superiors; she must not complain, lest she become an object of complaint; she must not ask somebody else to do anything for her that is not absolutely indispensable; she must do all she can for others without waiting to be asked; she must learn to like what she dislikes, bear the unbearable, even be pleased by it and seek it. One of Thérèse's neighbors in choir rattled her rosary continuously, and the irritating noise made recollection almost impossible, but Thérèse came to regard it as a sort of music, favorable to a special kind of prayer; she called it the "prayer of endurance."

She laughed with her novices but scolded them, too, fairly and in moderation. She never withdrew a reprimand or worried because she had to give pain — it must be left to have its effect, and "to run after one who has been chidden and console her does more harm than good." If she is left alone she has to humble herself and look to Heaven for help. Sister Thérèse said what she thought and did not go out of her way to make herself popular; she was prepared to be misunderstood and misrepresented. She was frank with the novices and expected them to be frank with her, allowing them to reprove her at need and point out her own deficiencies. If her authority suffered, Heaven had to make it good. She let them talk on, even when they hurt her or were tiresome with their boring outpourings.

The girls she had to deal with were often touchy, weak, or obstinate, but she never gave one up. Like Joan of Arc, she was fighting for Heaven: to God were due the victories; to herself, the defeats. A novice boasted of having won her point in a discussion. "Oh!" exclaimed Thérèse. "You are after success. That's a thing to be guarded against. It's better to say with our Lord, 'I seek not my own glory; there is one that seeketh and judgeth.' "

She did her duty of argument, warning, and appeal, and then left the intractable or troubled soul to the care of God. She stopped her classes at once when the bell rang, for observance of the rule was more efficacious than any words of hers. Once, at the signal for Office, she cut short the recital of a novice's troubles with the words, "God is calling you. He wants you to bear it by yourself."

The poor girl went away in deep dejection, but Thérèse's words to her had been a prayer to God, and during the Office, a strange peace came upon her and all doubts were dispelled. God finished what Sister Thérèse had begun.

Little by little, her self-imposed simplicity enabled her to be glad at her own insufficiency. When she failed to be of help to one of her daughters, hope would increase rather than diminish, for it was an indication that she must stand aside and let grace have free play; so she would aid it with her prayers and the offering up of her own humiliation.

She made enemies for herself — it could hardly be otherwise. There was bitterness and spite and complaints to be endured from her dear daughters as there had been from her dear sisters and dear mothers. She did all she could to overcome and disarm them with strict attention to the requirements of justice — and sometimes succeeded. All she had to give she gave, and asked in return that everything should be given to God. As the process of beatification shows, her gifts of sympathy and encouragement made for her good friends as well.

"He whom you have taken for your spouse," she would say, "is the perfection of perfectness; nevertheless He has one great infirmity, if I may dare say it — He is blind! And there is one thing He does not know — *arithmetic!* If He could see and calculate properly, our sins would surely constrain Him to annihilate us; but instead, His love for us makes Him positively blind . . . But to produce this blindness and prevent Him from making a simple addition sum, you must know how to capture His heart . . . That is His weak side." Advantage must not be taken of this divine weakness to sin with impunity; but if a sin is committed, then it must be trustfully confessed to Him with loving generosity, and after that put out of mind, when He will forget it too.

With such lessons as these did Thérèse oppose weariness, discouragement, or depression, but it is not at all certain that even the best and most intelligent of the novices appreciated her teaching at its full value. Her lively manner and unexpected turns of speech hid its depth from them. "Isn't she amusing!" was often their comment, and "We shan't laugh today" they would say when Sister Thérèse was absent from recreation.

At one evening recreation during the Christmastide of 1894, Thérèse was talking with her two elder sisters, Mother Agnes and Sister Mary, and evoking memories of Christmases that were past. She had an unusual memory and liked to recall events from the old days because they were a testimony of God's marvelous dealings with her. While she related them so vividly, her hearers had only to shut their eyes to see the house at Alençon, Les Buissonnets, their relatives and friends, and the little Thérèse with her big blue eyes and flying fair hair, merry and melancholy by turns, emotional and reflective, generous, loving. That child was their sister, and it might well be would one day be a saint, as their father had foretold. As she listened, Sister Mary, moved by the recital and perhaps prompted by an angel of good counsel, exclaimed suddenly, "Mother Prioress, she ought to be told to write all these things down!" Why on earth? She would dissipate her mind with so many duties. Wasn't time enough wasted talking about herself without writing it as well? That was Thérèse's opinion of the suggestion, and Mother Agnes agreed. But Sister Mary pressed her point: proper piety toward the past, gratitude to the dead, edification of the community, and Heaven knows what else. It is quite certain that she brought forward some weighty argument of which we are ignorant, for eventually the prioress agreed and put Sister Thérèse under obedience to use her short leisure in this way. She even fixed a date for the delivery of the manuscript, in one year's time, on January 20, 1896.

First of all, Thérèse knelt and put this work into the hands of our Lady, "so that she should not write a line that would be disagreeable to her." Then she took a school exercise book, balanced on a small desk on her knee, and, in level precise writing, began the simple autobiography which was one day to reveal her holiness to the whole world. It was not a matter of producing literature; she was only concerned to provide her sisters in blood, and perhaps a few others, with an occasion for loving God more by the perusal of all that He had done for her. With such readers in view, she adopted the tone of a little girl talking to her grownup elders, and she carried ingenuousness to its limit. The pages are covered with the floweriness that they liked and the sighs, effusions, and pious aspirations which appealed to them and might help their prayers. Recollections fall over one another; she pours them out as she goes along and then has to turn back to finish them; there is no sign of any elaborated plan — it is just the overflowing of a soul.

That is both the weakness and the charm of the first part of *The Story of a Soul,* which ends with Céline's entry into Carmel, but already toward the end, her tone alters and the style becomes more staid. Thérèse writes with a different pen and another ink when she continues her reminiscences for Mother Mary of Gonzaga, after that lady had again become prioress. It must not be forgotten that the first part was addressed to Pauline, the "little mother," so that Thérèse's affection for her is continually being mixed up with the spiritual outpourings. She had also very little time for writing; she was not dispensed from any of her regular duties, and had at most two hours to spare from choir-office, meditation, the novitiate, attending the hatch, painting, sweeping, writing hymns, sometimes laundry-work, and always interruptions to be reckoned with. What would a "literary gent" say to working in such conditions?

Moreover, Sister Thérèse put the whole of herself into what she was doing, whatever its relative interest, difficulty, or importance, persuaded that a floor well scrubbed for His sake is as pleasing to God as a fervent prayer. People have been worn out with less; she wore herself out, she wanted to: she aimed at self-annihilation. At twenty-two, Teresa had attained the perfection of a great saint and, however surprising it may be, nobody but her sisters had an inkling of it. She could not be seen "being good," or rather, she seemed to have only to let herself be; it was thought that there was no merit in it, that her nature carried her along. People could not see the strife in which she was still ceaselessly engaged; her equanimity concealed it. Because she was always smiling it was supposed that she was "full of consolations." Some envied her. Others — the few who realized it — were frightened by her abnegation and refused to admire it, lest they, too, should be compelled to follow her example. They found it safer to set her down as nice and negligible: a pleasant young nun, careful of the rule — who managed the novices well, told stories splendidly, painted pretty pictures, and wrote pretty poems; there was no question of her being a saint.

Thérèse had obtained what she had aimed at: the nuns ignored her. Nor, although He was her sole confidant, did God know her either — or, rather He pretended not to. That was what made Thérèse throw herself at Him with such audacity. The more He hid Himself, the more she wanted Him; the more He ignored her, the more she made an offering of herself.

On the other hand, her forsakenness must not be exaggerated, for there are certain admissions made privately to Mother Agnes, apparently while Thérèse was still a novice. "Several times in the garden in summer," she says, "after the beginning of the 'great silence' in the evening, I have been in so complete a state of recollection, my heart so at one with God, and making acts of love so warmly and yet *without any effort*, that it seems to me these graces were what our mother St. Teresa calls 'flights of the spirit' . . . I felt, as it were, a veil hung between me and earthly reality, and our Lady's cloak covered me completely. I had ceased to belong to this world, and I did all I had to do . . . as if my body were only lent to me for the purpose." Thérèse would live in deep peace for several days under the influence of such exceptional graces; then she would "wake up."

During Mass on the feast of the Holy Trinity, June 9, 1895, Thérèse made with special fervor her "act of offering as a burnt-sacrifice to the *merciful love of our God*." Divine justice needs a sacrificial victim — but who ever thinks of trusting to His love? "He is misunderstood and repudiated everywhere." Human hearts turn to other created beings, "seeking their happiness in an affection so weak that it cannot endure a moment." "O God, shall Your rejected love remain within Your own heart?" Would He not joyfully consume souls in its fire and cease to have infinite tenderness confined within His own breast? If He is glad at the satisfying of His justice which regards only this world, "how much more of His love of mercy which reaches to the heavens!" "Jesus," she exclaimed, "*may I be that happy victim!*"

But a religious is not at liberty to hand herself over in this deliberate way even to God without the permission of her superior. It is possible that Mother Agnes regarded this act of immolation as superfluous and of no importance, a childlike fancy, when she smilingly approved it. To bind herself more surely, Thérèse wrote down her offering and submitted its terms to the judgment of a theologian, as a will is shown to a solicitor; then she put the paper between the pages of the Testament that she always carried with her.

The glory of God and of His Church, the salvation and deliverance of souls, the fulfilling of the divine will: these were her objects; and to them she added that "she might be a saint." But here Thérèse was conscious of her own helplessness and she asked that God "would be Himself her holiness," offering the merits of our Lord and of His mother and the other saints, and beseeching Jesus to "take away from her the freedom to displease Him." She hoped for Heaven, but would not "collect merits" in order to win it: God's love, God's approval, God's comfort: it was just those that she wanted; she would be the martyr of divine love. "May this martyrdom prepare me to appear before You and at my death bear me straight to the eternal embrace of Your merciful love . . . I want this offering to be repeated endlessly every time my heart beats, O my Well-beloved, until, when the darkness has fled away, I can tell my love face-to-face forever." Her signature is followed by the words "An unworthy Carmelite nun."

She often repeated this act of oblation, but kept it secret except from two of the novices; the others might have laughed.

The fire of love so much desired was to envelop her with a mystical and even some sort of physical reality, like the dart with which the seraph pierced the heart of Teresa of Avila. A few days later, as she was about to make the Stations of the Cross, she suddenly felt herself "struck so burningly by a shaft of fire that I thought I should die." She could find no comparison to illustrate the "intense heat of this flame. Some invisible power seemed to surround me wholly with fire. What burning, and what delight! . . . A minute, a second, more of it, and my soul would have left my body."

She fell back *at once* into her accustomed aridity. But Love had come to her, and for the future she could live, in the words of Father Martin, "in the ceaseless exercise of charity" without experiencing its delights. They did not matter, for she was no longer Thérèse; Jesus lived and felt in her, and it must be Him alone.

Chapter Ten

Sickness

Sister Thérèse thought she ought to tell Mother Agnes of Jesus of Divine Love's high ravishment of her, but her sister seems not to have been impressed. Nor did she take any notice of *The Story of a Soul* when it was faithfully delivered to her on bended knee as the nuns were going into choir on the eve of St. Agnes. It was put aside to be read another time, for Mother Agnes had plenty of other things to think about. Her three years of office were nearly over, and all her attention was required to superintend the election of a good and prudent successor. Prayer alternated with confabulations, and a taste for intrigue showed itself among the less worthy religious. There were two parties: one — I will not call it the "Martin party," for, as I have said above, there was no such thing — was in favor of the re-election of Mother Agnes; the other (indubitably anti-Martin) wanted Mother Mary of Gonzaga back again, because of her age and experience. It is quite likely that the former prioress was not at all content with having had to play second fiddle; indeed, she let both Mother Agnes and Sister Thérèse know more than once that she did not regard herself as superseded and was still "all there." At the election, there were seven scrutinies, and eventually Mother Mary of Gonzaga gained the required majority of votes. It may be asserted that Thérèse voted for her, for she was always on the side that looked from a human point of view less favorably disposed toward herself. That Mother Agnes was not re-elected was providential, for it would never have done for her to have been in a position to ease Thérèse's last years and then bring forward the cause of her beatification: malicious tongues would certainly have alleged that the Martin sisters under the direction of Pauline had conspired for the glorification of one of their family.

Mother Mary at once demonstrated her impenitent "imperialism." She decided to retain the name and office of novice-mistress, although delegating its direct exercise; she did not remove Thérèse, whom she valued, but kept her well under her hand, and, as prioress, her will was again law. So did Sister Thérèse continue on the road of her sanctification.

Au monde, quel bonheur extrême!
J'ai dit un éternel adieu.
Elevé plus haut que lui-même
Mon coeur n'a d'autre appui que Dieu.
Et maintenant, je le proclame,
Ce que j'estime près de lui,
C'est de voir mon coeur et mon âme
Appuyés sans aucun appui.[12]

The first onset of illness was fierce, but when it came, it caused Thérèse no surprise. Her body had shared the fatigue, the privation, and the suffering of her soul, with other burdens added. It was

[12]*Poésies de Soeur Thérèse: Glose sur le Divin,* d'après St. Jean de la Croix (1896).

only to be expected that such a life would be too much for the physical constitution of a young girl, however robust she might be: fasting, the discipline, choir-office, hours of kneeling; household work, going up and down steep staircases twenty times a day, the enduring of heat and cold (the house was very damp); she might not lean against anything when she was tired or lie down even in her own cell, and had to keep a bold and cheerful front, at the same time refusing to ask or accept any dispensation or relaxation; on top of all this, she had less food and sleep than she needed. This daily overworking gradually bore Sister Thérèse down, but when she realized it, she could not make up her mind to admit it. When going upstairs and not seen by anyone, she clung to the banisters, she fell asleep during her prayers, and was short of breath and sweated and was frozen by the slightest draught. She was cold, always and everywhere, for the whole seven years that she was in the convent except for a month or two in summer (only in the depth of winter was there a fire in the recreation-room, and she wouldn't go too near to that); seven years of cold, overwork, and nervous exhaustion was the record of her body, and she had so carefully hidden its effects that nobody put her under obedience to take some rest.

She endured two months of the trying rule of Mother Mary of Gonzaga, who had again given her the sacristy work. Then, in the night of April 3, after the long offices of Maundy Thursday, at a moment when she thought she was "stronger than ever," she heard "a far-away sound telling her of the coming of the Bridegroom." That is a figure of speech; the plain fact is this: seeing that she was tired, the prioress forbade her to watch all night before the altar of repose and sent her to bed at midnight. Thérèse's head was hardly on the pillow when she "felt something very hot and wet rise into her mouth." She thought she was going to die, and her "heart jumped with joy," but she did not light her lamp and, "restraining her curiosity till the morning," went quietly to sleep. When she got up at five on Good Friday, she found that her handkerchief was soaked in blood. She assisted fervently at prime and the chapter meeting, and then went to tell the prioress; she was feeling neither ill nor tired. Mother Mary was doubtless rather disturbed, but she gave permission to Thérèse to go on with her Holy Week observances, and she bore the Good Friday fast and offices without apparent harm; she even cleaned the windows, refusing the proffered help of a novice who was frightened by her pallor. The next night, she brought up more blood, but she went on with her work without troubling about it.

Early in the morning of May 10, she had a dream. She seemed to be walking in a gallery with the prioress, when they met three Carmelites wearing their great veils and white cloaks. They seemed to have come from Heaven. One of them lifted her veil, and Sister Thérèse recognized her as Mother Anne of Jesus, the companion of St. Thérèse and foundress of Carmel in France. Her lovely face seemed to be "lit up with its own light," and Thérèse asked her, "Is God going to fetch me away soon?"

"Very soon," replied Mother Anne.

"Doesn't He ask anything of me except my poor little deeds and intentions?"

"Nothing else."

"Is He pleased with me?"

"Very pleased."

Mother Anne leaned forward to embrace her, and Thérèse woke up.

So far, she had told none of her three sisters of her threatening health, but when she developed a hard insistent cough, they soon noticed it, warned the prioress, and two doctors were called in.

One of them was Joan Guérin's husband. Their examination detected nothing seriously wrong; their treatment got rid of the cough, color came back to her cheeks, and for a few months, Thérèse was able to carry on with her duties. "You ask news of my health," she wrote to Léonie on July 12. "Well, my cough has quite gone. Does that satisfy you? But it won't prevent God from taking me when He wills. I do my best to be nothing but a little child, so I don't have to make a lot of preparations. Jesus Himself will pay my fare and the cost of going into Heaven." In the same letter she quotes the *Song of Songs:* "How is it possible to be afraid of Him who tells us that His heart is held 'with one hair of our neck'?"

She tried to be as patient as she could. "The road of sickness is a very long one," she said to a novice, "I rely solely on love."

When she was freed from the cares of office, Mother Agnes of Jesus had been able to find time to go over the manuscript that had been written for her. She was only half-convinced by it, but it at least made clear the exceptional quality of the soul she had formed, or at any rate inspired, in the old days at Les Buissonnets. Presumably she showed that precious exercise-book to her elder sister, for during September, Mary, with permission of the prioress, asked Thérèse to set down for her an account of the "little way." The request did not have to be pressed, and Thérèse wrote straight off those burning pages that make up the eleventh chapter of *The Story of a Soul,* which in order of time comes nine months before the two preceding ones.

After a graceful compliment to the godmother who had given her to the Lord at the font, she hymns the fiery furnace of love and the sole path that leads thereto — abandonment of self into the arms of God.

> Love is proved by deeds. What are a little child's deeds? It offers flowers, which it finds among the thorns and in the grass of its tiniest actions. God gives us His love extravagantly, but what extravagance can be expected from a tiny creature made to crawl about on the ground? She must wed herself to the "folly" of God and borrow from the Eagle His own mighty wings and with them fly up to Him one day. This is not a rash ambition. Nothing is too small for the Infinite Mercy, and were it possible for God to find a poorer soul than hers, He would fill it with correspondingly greater blessings, provided it was entirely given up to Him.

Sister Thérèse had a special veneration for a young martyr in Tonkin, whose simplicity had attracted her, Blessed Théophane Venard (d. 1861), and she was joined in friendship with two young missionaries, ordained together, who had appealed for her help. She prayed for them, wrote to them, and joined from afar in their labors. The idea of the conversion of the whole world had always obsessed her. Now she learned that two months ago, there had been a requisition for a capable nun to be sent to the Carmel at Hanoi in French Indo-China — and her name had come up for consideration. The notion of taking her prayers and sacrifices and love into the heart of a heathen land and perhaps risking martyrdom was indeed a temptation, and when the matter was mooted again, she began to hope to get better enough to go and die there. This was in November, and she began a novena to Blessed Théophane; but before it was finished, a sudden relapse showed that God willed otherwise.

She could not digest her food and was continually feverish, but neither fever nor exhaustion could make her falter. She took part in all the community exercises and would excuse herself from none of her personal observances, keeping up the struggle on two fronts at once, against her soul and against her body; wherever and whenever she was needed, there she was, punctual and cheerful. No one thought of pitying her any more than she thought of pitying herself. So she got through the winter up to the Epiphany of 1897, when she made a cantata on the Flight into Egypt to the air of *Les gondolières vénitiennes* and the Credo from the opera *Herculanum*. She still taught and smiled on the novices, and encouraged her sisters, of whom even the elder ones now came to her for advice.

But her strength was going rapidly, and the ability to keep up its semblance suddenly left her. Her heart failed at "the violent effort she had to make to stand up and chant" at the evening office; soon she was unable to go upstairs by herself, stopping to get breath on each step; it took her an hour to undress; she lay awake most of the night, her teeth chattering with fever; and every morning, she faced afresh the relentless rigor of the rule she had chosen. She persevered until Lent and then, all at once, collapsed completely.

The doctor knew Thérèse was doomed, and said so, and Mother Mary of Gonzaga had at last to submit to the evidence. A last medical effort was made; she was still allowed downstairs, but had to pass long hours in her cell, where she was subjected to a very painful treatment.

"Does it hurt you very much, Sister Thérèse?"

"Yes; but I've always wanted to suffer." And she preferred her cell to the infirmary, for there she could suffer alone. "When I'm pitied and spoiled, I'm no longer happy," she declared.

The whole convent knew that Sister Thérèse was going to die. She heard the kitchen-sister wondering what the mother prioress would find to write in her obituary notice. "She came here, she lived here, she was taken ill, and she died," and that indeed was all there was to be said — except that those things were or would be done in the perfection of charity.

Mother Agnes of Jesus had become absolutely convinced that Thérèse was a saint, and she now noted down from day to day the more striking of her sayings; later on, these formed the most precious book of *Novissima verba.* From May to September 30, it is like a spiritual diary, but only of as much as a strong and sensitive soul was willing to say. The worst was kept for herself and God; she told of her poor little joys and was silent about her real troubles. By trying to read between the lines, we may be able to get some idea of the depths in which she was.

She welcomed our Lady's month with a smile, and tried to be serene. Somebody had spoken of man's ingratitude. Thérèse looked for no earthly recognition, but "the hope of heavenly reward? She would have no more in Heaven, for she was with God already." "If God renders to every man according to his works He will find her a difficult problem . . . He will have to render to her according to His own works." "Really it would be better if God did not know whose was the little love she had given Him, so that He wouldn't have to reward her for it."

She had hoped to be faithfully in harness to the end, but now all her duties had been taken from her and she kept some small piece of work always nearby so as not to waste her time. One morning, she has two small difficulties, which account for her cheerfulness.

> Was she afraid of death? She was not at all sure of herself. Anyway, she did not rely on her own thoughts: God would either give her fear or not. She had tried to show she was brave by keeping on telling Him that she was. One must not make people tell lies.

She knew exactly when the attempted medical remedies were useless and sent them in spirit to sick missionaries who had neither time nor means to look after themselves.

On June 4, Thérèse thought the end had come and said farewell to her three sisters. For their sake, she would have liked to have a "beautiful death," but feared she ought not to — "See how our Lord died!" She was ready to welcome anything, even death without the sacraments, for everything may be a means of grace.

But she recovered a little and, as she could swallow better, was allowed Communion. After this, she found again the gift of tears that she had lost for so long; sitting in the garden, she watched some chicks beneath the wings of a white hen and wept gently, for they reminded her of our Lord's words in the Temple before His Passion.[13] Then she was able to walk again and offered up her walking for the missionaries.

Toward the end of May, she had made a first allusion to a "test of her soul" — namely, temptations *against faith* — and a month later, they were much worse. "My soul feels banished. Heaven is shut to me." But by a curious contradiction, it was at this very time that she said, "You will not lose by my death, for I shall send down a shower of roses."

Mother Agnes of Jesus had told the prioress that she had a manuscript of Thérèse's memories that would one day interest the community and suggested that they should be finished by the addition of some riper reflections on community life, if Thérèse were not too weak to do it. The prioress agreed and, when Thérèse asked what she should write, told her to write about charity and about the novices.

[13]Matt. 23:37.

So she set to work, sitting in a bath-chair under the chestnut trees in fine weather, writing what came into her mind, slowly, in big letters, wide spaces between the lines. It was her last testament, and forms the ninth and tenth chapters of *The Story of a Soul.* With humility and forgiveness, she addresses them to Mother Mary of Gonzaga, thanking her for the severity that had caused her so much pain. She confesses her only ambition, "to be a saint," the disproportion between her abilities and her ambition, the impossibility of attaining it by greatness and the consequent necessity of making use of small things; seeing it was an age of inventions, she would go up to God "by the lift." We already know part of her story, that of her illness; these pages lighten up the depths of her soul wherein the supreme test or trial was going on.

She had always longed for "the world to come," the promised land of the faithful and patient and humble and loving. A fleeting smile from our Lady had showed her a glimpse of it. Later on, a lightning-flash to her heart had made her experience for a moment a little of the ecstasy of love that is the portion of the righteous: the flame had gone out, but she could still dream of it. Her glowing steadfast faith had enabled her to enjoy Heaven without seeing it and without receiving any enlightenment, encouragement, or sensible sweetness.

That faith itself was now hidden, lost in mists that covered her soul so that she could no longer even see the "reflection of her dear heavenly home." Her heart, "weary of darkness," endeavored to find some rest "in the strengthening remembrance of an eternal life to come," but the darkness itself "borrowed the voice of the wicked" and mocked at her: "Do you dream of light and a fragrant home, the eternal possession of the almighty Creator? Go on! Go on! Death will lead you to yet deeper night . . ." It will be "the night of nothingness."

Thérèse stopped; she was on the verge of blasphemy. God forgive her! She had not "the delight of faith," but every day she did its works. "I have made more acts of faith during the past year than in all the rest of my life."

She fled from the tempter to Jesus; she was ready to give her life in confession of the faith that eluded her; she even declared that she was happy — since it was her Lord's good pleasure — "not to be able to contemplate on earth the beauties of the Heaven that awaited her" even with the eyes of faith.

Thérèse did not exaggerate this night of the spirit. "It is no longer a *curtain; it* is a *wall* between me and the starry firmament." "I feel no joy when I sing of the happiness of Heaven and the eternal possession of God, for I am singing only of that *which I want to believe*."

An occasional ray of sunshine, "a very little ray," relieved this heavy night, but it would pass at once and "leave the darkness thicker than before." Nevertheless, she continued in peace. She now believed only by an effort of will, but she believed. Love actually increased, and so did hope. "They [the angels and saints] want to see just how far my hope will stretch."

And charity toward her neighbor flourished. There was a certain nun whom Thérèse found disagreeable in every way. Not content with overcoming a natural antipathy, she set herself to treat her just as she would one of whom she was very fond. Whenever they met, Thérèse prayed for her; she did for her whatever services she could; if the nun was vexatious, Thérèse gave her a charming smile and changed the subject: and all so convincingly that the nun asked one day, "Sister Thérèse, won't you tell me why you are so drawn to me?" Presumably Thérèse was able to satisfy her curiosity without offending and without lying.

It is difficult to speak of "*little* actions," "*little* sacrifices," a "*little* way" in the face of supernatural heroisms of this sort, and this was only one among very many. Martyrdom is less exacting, for it calls for only one triumph over the protest of the flesh. It may be said that the essence of the "little way" is to put "great deeds at the service of small things." Thérèse explains that it involves "denudation" when a soul feels itself at breaking-point; the giving up of everything one has of one's own, even intellectual goods (personal expressions or ideas used without acknowledgment by somebody else) and spiritual goods, for it is of their nature to be a source of grace to others; patience in improvement, because God bestows His light only by degrees; the renouncement of all happiness, even spiritual happiness. Sister Thérèse was perfected in fullness, for she had absolutely nothing.

She wrote at length of her novices and all she had learned from them, of her two missionary "brothers," and the supreme revelation she received from Heaven upon the apostolate: the true apostle does not trouble about such and such a method of gaining souls; if he really loves God, running after Him, as the Canticle says, "to the odor of His ointments," souls will follow Him, for love attracts love.

At the beginning of July, the work was interrupted, for Thérèse became too weak to hold her pen, and both words and thoughts were failing. Renewed blood-spitting caused her to be taken to the infirmary, to the white-curtained bed in which she was to die, and she joyfully gave up her beloved cell — she had still something to give after all!

She ransacked her conscience in expectation of receiving the last sacraments; when she came to sins of the senses, she accused herself of having once, when traveling, used "a bottle of *eau de cologne* with too much pleasure" — perhaps that was why she was suffering so much now! When the superior came to see her, she received him with such a bright and reposeful face that he decided the last sacraments were not yet called for, while some of the nuns did not believe she was likely to die at all.

People kept on asking her questions. Did she fear eternal punishment? "Little children are not damned," she murmured. Was she glad of the benefit that individuals would certainly draw later on from her books? "Obviously everything comes from God, and if I derive any glory from it, the credit won't be mine." She was ready for her writings to be thrown into the fire. "What would you do if you had to begin life all over again?" somebody asked. "It seems to me that I should do just what I have done," she replied simply. This was not self-satisfaction and incurable pride, but enlightenment — truth proceeding from the mouth of a babe. Her bruised and disturbed spirit gave vent to flashes not her own, as when she declared with stunning assurance that "God will have to do whatever I want in Heaven because I have never followed my own will on earth!"

Surely never to have done one's own will, without a shadow of material constraint upon it, is a supreme triumph for that will.

Her assurance went further yet.

"You will look down on us from above?"

"No. I shall *come* down."

By the eve of the feast of Our Lady of Mount Carmel, Thérèse was a living skeleton. "How glad I am to see myself being destroyed!" However, she would be able to receive Communion tomorrow. Would she be called after that? Did anyone think so? "Shall I leave my little way in order to die?" On July 17, there was more light: the conqueror, chosen by God from all others, became conscious of her election and the powers that He had given her.

"I believe that my mission is about to begin . . . If my wishes are granted, my Heaven will be spent on earth until the end of the world . . . I want to spend my Heaven doing good on earth . . . I shan't be able to rest so long as there are souls to be saved. But when the angel says, 'Time is no more,' then I shall rest and be happy, for the tale of the chosen will be complete." What a prophecy in so small a mouth! "Would God give me this wish if He did not intend to realize it?" She was a "very brave soldier," and it was not pleasure at the prospect of release from the trials of life that drew her on, but "To love and be loved, and to come back to earth to make Love loved."

In this expectation and certitude, Thérèse continued to expend the fruits of her charity — devoid of the consolations of faith — upon her superiors and companions and novices. It was washing-day, and very hot. So! She must suffer much in order that their burdens might be eased . . .

The hemorrhages were so much worse by the end of the month that at last she was anointed and given the Viaticum, asking forgiveness of all the community for her trespasses. Afterward, the inopportune visit of several nuns interrupted her thanksgiving. When our Lord withdrew to pray by Himself, crowds followed Him, and He did not send them away. So, then, did Sister Thérèse leave her God that she might greet her importunate sisters pleasantly.

Somebody saw fit to bring into the infirmary the pallet upon which her dead body was to be laid out. Thérèse burst out laughing. She had never been comfortable in her body and always found it a nuisance: it was high time she was out of it.

Chapter Eleven

Thérèse Is Glorified

The disease was developing — constant vomiting, suffocation, loss of consciousness. Still Thérèse struggled on. Was she dying of not being able to die, like her Spanish namesake? That is nature's instinct, but grace murmurs, "May God's will be done." Oh, she never thought herself a great saint! It had been God's good pleasure to make her the vessel of certain things that did good, and would go on doing it: good to herself and to others, especially others. It was not her business to look further. Her happiness was to recognize her imperfection; but she was anxious to know whether she really was humble of heart, and to get that certainty, she wanted to go on being humiliated and ill-treated.

Sister Genevieve (Céline) had thoughtfully been made assistant infirmarian to be near her sister, and Thérèse was afraid that her incessant cough would wake her up at night — that was all she had against the spasms that tore her.

On August 6, she was so bad that she could only say, "If one only knew! . . ." and "What would it be did I not love God?" They thought she was patient. Not she! She had never had a minute's patience in her life. That patience was not *hers*. She did not hide her atrocious sufferings; if at least she were bearing them well!

A fortnight later, she received the Viaticum for the last time. The low sound of the *Miserere* alone was enough to make her faint. She felt she had "lost her ideas," and called on our Lady to hold her head in her hands. There was not a bit of her body that was not in agony, and she begged for prayers. But immediately they were said, she refused their effects, offering them instead for those sinners who needed them so much more. When her sufferings were beyond human endurance, she recanted and accepted them with a sense of shame. What could she complain of? Was not God giving her "exactly as much as she could bear"? — of which the best proof is that she bore it.

On the 25th, she fell suddenly into a state of unspeakable distress. "We *must* pray for the dying! Oh, if people only knew!" and then "I am making a terrible fuss — but I don't want to suffer less." Thirst was added to her afflictions.

Jesus had said, "I thirst," and when she was offered iced water, Thérèse said, "Oh, how I want this! . . . No, only a drop. My tongue is not parched enough!"

Two days later, she pointed out a dark hole in the garden under the chestnut trees. "I'm in a hole like that, soul and body . . . The darkness is awful; but I'm at peace." She had hardly the strength to make the Sign of the Cross. "O God, be pitiful to me! I've no more than that to say." But God seemed to have no pity.

On the anniversary of Thérèse's profession (September 8), a friend sent her a bunch of wildflowers, and a robin, flying in at the window, delighted her by hopping about the bed. She plaited two wreaths of cornflowers for the picture of the smiling Madonna. Then she received violets ("Ought she to smell them?") and next day a rose, the petals of which she scattered over the crucifix that never left her side. Then it was that she spoke those prophetic words: "Keep these petals carefully, sisters, and don't lose any of them. Later on, they will be useful to you for making people happy." "Now, I hope and believe, my exile is nearly over," she added, and when, one evening, a dove perched cooing on the windowsill, Pauline and Céline were reminded of the words of the Canticle: "Winter is now passed, the rain is over and gone . . . The voice of the turtle is heard in our land . . . Arise, my love, my beautiful one, and come!"[14]

These were only small exterior alleviations. The disease kept on its implacable way, until, on the morning of September 29, there were signs of imminent death.

"Is this the end?" Thérèse asked the prioress. "What must I do to die? I shall never know how to die."

Pauline read the office of St. Michael the Archangel to her and the prayers for the dying. The doctor came and confirmed the impression of the prioress.

"Is it today, Mother?"

"Yes."

When she heard one of the nuns say that "God is going to be very happy today," Thérèse exclaimed, "So am I," but her joy soon went; all that day she was torn with pain and fear of death, and the last night was awful. But in the midst of it, she was heard to sigh, "O God, yes, yes! *I will all this*."

She had reached perfection. The greedy snatching of her childhood was turned against herself, against her own will and self-esteem. She chose all this suffering, bodily torture, faintness of heart, spiritual uncertainty, without any ulterior motive of expected reward. She had attained the uttermost point where everything in her was

[14]Cant. 2:11-13 (RSV = Song of Sol. 2:11-13).

pain, deprivation, nothingness. The house was empty, the whole of it at the disposal of divine grace.

She prayed in vain; it was "unalloyed anguish, without a trace of relief or comfort," and it lasted through another day. She was restless, sitting up in bed, clinging to life with all her strength. "Perhaps this will go on for months! It will be worse tomorrow. All right, then — so much the better!" Then she fell back again.

"If this is the prelude, what can death itself be like? . . ."

"The cup is full to the brim . . ."

"O God, You are so good! Yes, I know You are good . . ."

About three o'clock in the afternoon, she stretched her arms out crosswise, with her eyes on an image of Our Lady of Mount Carmel, and said to the prioress, "Present me to our Lady, quickly, and get me ready to die well."

Mother Mary of Gonzaga calmed and reassured her, speaking of trust in God's loving-kindness and of her own humility; this time Thérèse did not deny it, but said with lovely simplicity, "I do not regret having given myself up to Love."

The very next minute, pain drew from her the cry, "I would never have believed it possible to suffer so much." "I can't breathe, and I can't die," and so, hanging between life and death, she renewed her offering: "I am quite willing to go on suffering."

About five o'clock, Mother Agnes, who was then alone with Thérèse, saw a sudden change come over her face. She had the passing-bell rung, and the whole community hurried to the infirmary. Thérèse smiled at each one and then turned her eyes to the crucifix; she was plainly *in extremis*, but the agony was long. When the *Angelus* rang at six, she looked up beseechingly at the "smiling Madonna"; at seven, the prioress dismissed the bystanders.

"Isn't it the end yet, Mother? No matter! I don't want to cut short my sufferings," and she turned again to her crucifix: "I love Him . . . O God, I love You . . ."

The next moment, her head fell gently backward. She seemed to be dead, and the prioress summoned the nuns. As they knelt around the bed, Sister Thérèse's face "regained the lily-whiteness that it had when she was well"; her eyes were fixed but still alive, looking upward and shining with an unearthly happiness. "She made certain movements with her head," says Mother Agnes, "as though she were several times struck by a shaft of love." It would certainly seem to have been an ecstasy and lasted the space of a *Credo*. Then Thérèse closed her eyes and died. It was about twenty past seven in the evening of September 30, 1897; she was twenty-four years and nine months old.

Once, when shown a photograph of herself, Thérèse had said with a smile, "Yes, that's the envelope. When will anyone see the letter inside? I should like to see that letter."

Now at last she knew. That letter, inspired, worked over, and finished off by her Lord, was before Almighty God, and it seems that it was His will that its message should be at once spread throughout the face of the earth; the young warrior, victor over herself, was given the whole world in which to enlarge her conquests. From her brown scapular as from an apron, she scattered roses like rain — not roses of paper or plaster or china or marble, but living ones, white or blood-red, roses of suffering and sacrifice and innocence (any self-respecting artist would hesitate at representing them); and in her hand, she bore a banner with two devices, the smiling face of the Child and the agonized face of the Crucified. She did not call for a mawkish veneration; she did not put forward a soft and feeble example; everything was strong; she was of the stock of Catherine of Siena and Joan of Arc, and her "little way" was a heroic way — nothing less than plenary love of God and total surrender to Him, down to the least thoughts and actions; to become as a little child is to put oneself through the mill.

Imitation flowers and sham simplicity, products of an emotionalism that becomes sheer sentimentality, ought to be stripped from the devotion accorded to one from whom God withheld sensible consolation for almost the whole of her life. The figure of the "shower of roses" has served its turn, and served it well in winning over the many who have a taste for the romantic and pretty. But these "roses" are in fact graces, and grace is not carried easily: for complete fruition, it requires a martyrdom of the soul.

Wrapped in her big white cloak, a chaplet of white roses on her head and a palm branch in her hand, the body of Sister Thérèse lay with face uncovered behind the chapel grating, where her relatives and friends, known and unknown, could see her for the last time. The death of a cloistered nun is not very important, but in a small town, even in one of religious tepidity like Lisieux, it is quite an event, especially if the nun was young and a native of the place by birth or residence.

During her conventual life, Sister Thérèse had been misunderstood by many of her fellows and an object of jealousy and petty persecution for two or three, but her lingering death and final triumph had made a sensation among them. Some thought they could smell the fragrance of lilies and violets around the body; a lay-sister, who had treated her rather badly, in a paroxysm of remorse pressed her forehead against the dead feet, and was straightway cured of an acute anemia. Doubtless this was bruited in the town, and it is probable that for some time, the kitchen-sister had been unable to refrain from chattering about "our little saint" when she went shopping. She may have been believed or not, but the fact that the dead nun was the youngest child of M. Martin, who had given five daughters to religion and this one when she was only fifteen, was enough to provoke sympathetic interest and curiosity, at any rate among the devout.

Many visited the chapel, and their medals and rosaries touched the holy body, but only a few, apart from relatives and some of the neighboring clergy, followed the coffin up the steep and tree-lined road to the municipal cemetery. While the Carmelites prayed in choir, Sister Thérèse was taken from them and buried in a corner of the plot reserved for religious on one of the upper terraces. A wooden cross was set over the grave inscribed with her name and her promise: *Je passerai mon ciel à faire du bien sur la terre*. Today its place is taken by a cenotaph, for, of course, the body is no longer there, but it is a good place to go and meditate, amid the peace and richness of that lovely part of Normandy. For a time the mother earth which Thérèse had loved so much, and whose joys she had renounced, was in possession of her frail body; but within two years, petitions, offerings, and thanks were accumulating on the grave in the form of letters, crosses, rosaries, and other *ex-votos*. It was there that her public *cultus* was born.

Her death was transfiguring the Lisieux Carmel. The mistrustful were convinced, the hostile disarmed, and in their grief, the nuns recovered a sisterly unanimity. The character of the prioress herself was modified. She was now quite sure of Thérèse's holiness and asserted that, while praying before her picture, Thérèse spoke to her. The prioress tells us no more about this, except that "I alone know all I owe her!" Instead of the ordinary obituary notice to all the other Carmels, Mother Mary of Gonzaga decided to send out copies of *The Story of a Soul*, with an account of Thérèse's last hours added. It was accordingly printed, and in the following October, the book began to tell her name, her life, and her promises to Carmelites throughout the world. It was translated and circulated, and there soon came a day when there was no friend of Carmel who did not know of God's gift to that order which had been born beneath the mantle of Elijah and reformed by the great Thérèse. So it was decided to make the book public.

Its effect was swift and strong, and a stream of postulants began to flow to Lisieux, from France, Ireland, Italy, Portugal, and Argentina. It was more than could be coped with, and many of them overflowed into other convents. There were some remarkable souls among them: Lisieux will not forget Sister Mary Angela, Sister Thérèse of the Eucharist, or Sister Thérèse of the Sacred Heart, the first of whom became prioress. The clergy were no less impressed; everywhere they were talking about this holy child; but the inspirations and miracles of her worldwide apostolate were already spreading in advance of them. She had said, "I will come down," and she had spoken truly.

I do not intend to sum up, even briefly, Thérèse's "second life" on earth and her intimate relations with the living during the past thirty-six years. Up to date, the succinct accounts of marvels of help, healing, conversion, forewarning, and vision fill seven volumes, entitled *Showers of Roses* — and they form only a drop in the torrent of testimonies that ceaselessly flows into the convent at Lisieux. Sister Thérèse is everywhere, and her solicitude passes nobody by: a male religious of considerable spiritual attainments in his sixty-sixth year begins his apprenticeship to perfection all over again, under her guidance; a young priest is instantaneously cured of advanced tuberculosis and henceforward has perfect health; a blind girl sees Sister Thérèse and at once recovers normal sight; the prioress of an Italian convent, unable to meet her bills, finds sufficient money in an empty desk; a Presbyterian minister in Edinburgh is led by her into the Church and goes to live in her old house at Alençon; an English industrialist, unjust to his workmen, becomes their friend and benefactor, and even their religious teacher, overnight; a child is saved from fire and a motor-car held back on the edge of a cliff by people calling on Thérèse; one of the petals from her crucifix banishes a cancer of the tongue; here, she comes in person to give a snowdrop to a child in pain and to save his mother from death; there, her statue in a hut encourages a number of pagans to cast down their idols. There is scarcely a country that has not seen her benefactions or where her name is not invoked: her holiness is clear, her miracles undeniable. The voice of the people is heard crying out on every hand.

In August 1910, an "informative process" was begun by the episcopal *curia* of Bayeux, which lasted a year. On December 10, 1913, the Congregation of Sacred Rites approved Thérèse's writings. On June 10, 1914, Pius X, that holy pope, "introduced her cause." War broke out, and Thérèse was not wanting. She also was in the trenches, protecting here, consoling there, prompting this man to leave his dug-out a moment before it collapsed, taking the hand of that one when he "went over the top." She encouraged the ranks, counseled the leaders, bent over the dying; thousands believe they owe their life to her, and still more their faith: flying-men, foot-sloggers, gunners, stretcher-bearers, French for the most part. No one will grudge her love for her own country and solicitude for its people when they were threatened. But a soul is a soul, and a man is a man. A Bavarian who had lost both legs was dying among his opponents, and the French chaplain suggested he should ask for the intercession of Sister Thérèse; the man had never heard of her, but complied with alacrity. Thérèse showed herself visibly to his eyes, and his life was saved. Thus, she made an apostle who carried the evidence of her benefits back from France to his own country.

Strengthened with new matter, the cause was continued after the war. On August 14, 1921, Benedict XV declared that Sister Thérèse had manifested heroic virtue. On February 11, 1923, Pius XI authorized the decree of approval of miracles, and on April 29, her beatification was proclaimed amid wild enthusiasm: Rome had suspended the regulation that stood in the way of so quick an official recognition. Henceforward Blessed Thérèse would have her feast-day and its appropriate Mass in all the churches depending on Bayeux and every Carmelite church and chapel in the world.

That was not enough for her; she could not agree to limit her ambition to the particular welfare of a small diocese or even of a great order. She had said, and she still said, "I choose all." The faithful at large wanted effect to be given to her importunity, she was multiplying miracles as she had multiplied penances, and at the end of two more years, a further process ended with her solemn canonization (May 17, 1925). From 1927, the liturgical *cultus* of this young girl is observed, on October 3,[15] in Catholic churches, under the name now deathlessly inscribed in Heaven of "Saint Thérèse of the Child Jesus and of the Holy Face," and as patroness of foreign missions and of all works for Russia. The first letter of her name really shines among the stars: she has overcome the world.

[15]The memorial of St. Thérèse is now observed on October 1.

Thérèse Is Glorified

There is no need to speak of the celebrations at Lisieux and the honors there accorded her, of the invasions by pilgrims, of the transformation of the convent chapel. The huge basilica, which will make manifest the enduring spiritual force of the "new Thérèse" is as yet hardly visible above ground; it will dominate the town (and unfortunately, the railway station), but it is still too early to estimate its beauty and fitness. The harm done by commerce to religion at Lisieux is a price that every place of pilgrimage has to pay; as for more tangible ugliness, it is pointless to refer to them again. Nevertheless, very many people find they never pray better than they do at Lisieux, for there they find the special help of the greatest saint of the modern age who, like another St. Francis, has given us a new gospel without modifying by jot or tittle the authentic Gospel of Jesus Christ. "Unless you be converted and become as little children . . ." "We are no longer children" is the reply, betraying our self-sufficiency, which has got to be broken. Thérèse will help. She broke her own self-sufficiency and complacency and her very existence; she broke her soul, spirit, heart, and body — with divine aid.

When Thérèse's coffin was opened on September 6, 1910, her body was not found to be incorrupt, as it is with so many saints; only the bones were left, and even they were already wasting, as if the destructive violence of her disease had attacked them, too. But some of the witnesses of the exhumation experienced a fragrance arising from this human dust, and it hung about the earth of the grave for several months. These relics were officially authenticated in 1917, and on March 26, 1923, they were translated with solemnity to the town in the presence of fifty thousand pilgrims. Before they were taken up, a woman from Angers set her paralytic child on the coffin; the little girl at once jumped up and was able to follow the procession, singing. There were three more miracles during its passage. Thus, the "nothingness" of Sister Thérèse came back to occupy the forever-famous convent wherein Love had burned her up, there to await in peace the victory of the last day.

Finished at Maisonneuve on October 18, 1933,
the feast of Luke the Evangelist, painter,
writer, physician of bodies and souls

Biographical Note

Henri Ghéon

(1875-1944)

Born Henri Vangeon, Henri Ghéon was a French playwright, critic, and poet. He was educated in Sens, but he moved to Paris to study medicine in 1893, when he began writing poetry. In 1909, he became a founding member of and a regular contributor to the French literary magazine *Nouvelle Revue Française* (NRF), "The New French Review."

While serving as a doctor in the army during the First World War, Ghéon returned to his Catholic faith and thereafter devoted much of his writing to the lives of the saints. His vivid descriptions of the saints and the times and places in which they lived bring these holy people to life for today's readers and inspire devotion to them and a desire to imitate their example.

Sophia Institute

Sophia Institute is a nonprofit institution that seeks to nurture the spiritual, moral, and cultural life of souls and to spread the Gospel of Christ in conformity with the authentic teachings of the Roman Catholic Church.

Sophia Institute Press fulfills this mission by offering translations, reprints, and new publications that afford readers a rich source of the enduring wisdom of mankind.

Sophia Institute also operates two popular online Catholic resources: CrisisMagazine.com and CatholicExchange.com.

Crisis Magazine provides insightful cultural analysis that arms readers with the arguments necessary for navigating the ideological and theological minefields of the day. *Catholic Exchange* provides world news from a Catholic perspective as well as daily devotionals and articles that will help you to grow in holiness and live a life consistent with the teachings of the Church.

In 2013, Sophia Institute launched Sophia Institute for Teachers to renew and rebuild Catholic culture through service to Catholic education. With the goal of nurturing the spiritual, moral, and cultural life of souls, and an abiding respect for the role and work of teachers, we strive to provide materials and programs that are at once enlightening to the mind and ennobling to the heart; faithful and complete, as well as useful and practical.

Sophia Institute gratefully recognizes the Solidarity Association for preserving and encouraging the growth of our apostolate over the course of many years. Without their generous and timely support, this book would not be in your hands.

www.SophiaInstitute.com
www.CatholicExchange.com
www.CrisisMagazine.com
www.SophiaInstituteforTeachers.org

Sophia Institute Press® is a registered trademark of Sophia Institute.
Sophia Institute is a tax-exempt institution as defined by the
Internal Revenue Code, Section 501(c)(3). Tax I.D. 22-2548708.